Girl
WORLD

HOW TO DITCH THE DRAMA AND FIND YOUR INNER AMAZING

Girl
WORLD

HOW TO DITCH THE DRAMA AND FIND YOUR INNER AMAZING

PATRICIA OTTAVIANO

sourcebooks
fire

Published by Sourcebooks Fire, an imprint of Sourcebooks, Inc.
P.O. Box 4410, Naperville, Illinois 60567–4410
(630) 961–3900
Fax: (630) 961–2168
www.sourcebooks.com

Library of Congress Cataloging-in-Publication Data

Ottaviano, Patricia.
  Girl world : how to ditch the drama and find your inner amazing / Patricia Ottaviano.
      pages cm
  Includes bibliographical references and index.
1. Self-esteem in adolescence--Juvenile literature. 2. Self-acceptance in adolescence--Juvenile literature. 3. Girls--Psychology--Juvenile literature. I. Title.
  BF724.3.S36O88 2015
  155.5'33--dc23

2015012961

Printed and bound in the United States of America.

VP 10 9 8 7 6 5 4 3 2 1

TO MY BEAUTIFUL MOTHER.
YOU HAVE ALWAYS BEEN AND WILL ALWAYS
BE MY VERY BEST FRIEND.
THANK YOU FOR YOUR UNCONDITIONAL LOVE.

CONTENTS

INTRODUCTION

Dear Girls,

Being a girl is harder than it looks. On one hand, we have our best friends by our sides to boost our happiness, give us a sense of belonging, lift us up on a bad day, and make us laugh until our stomachs hurt. Let's be real for a sec… It isn't always that pretty. Who hasn't experienced how downright mean girls can be? Who hasn't witnessed the judgment and negativity that can consume female conversation?

In a world where gossip, drama, and rumors seem to be never ending, of course there are going to be times when you doubt your friends, doubt yourself, and seriously start thinking that moving to a foreign country doesn't sound half bad.

What happens when you don't know who your

friends are anymore? Or when you don't know who to trust? Have you ever felt like insecurities, nerves, and uncertainties were ruling your world? Ever feel like everyone seems to have the missing piece to the puzzle but you? What about being the center of a hurtful rumor… Has that happened to you? Or how about experiencing some major FOMO (fear of missing out)? How do you pick yourself up after feeling torn down, left out, or straight-up rejected by girls you thought were your friends?

What if I told you that I've created a handbook, specially crafted for you, with *lots* of love, to navigate all of these circumstances and more?

Well, this is that book! It will guide you through Girl World, one sticky situation at a time, while pausing for advice breaks, some killer action steps, and perhaps an occasional dance party.

IN THIS GROOVY GUIDEBOOK YOU'LL LEARN…

- ♥ How to transform insecurities into strengths when feeling like you don't fit in or are the odd girl out.
- ♥ What to do if you feel nervous and intimidated by certain girls or when you don't trust your friends.
- ♥ Step-by-step ways to keep drama to a minimum when confrontations, conflicts, or arguments arise.

- ♥ How to handle the ugly side of social networking.
- ♥ How to fearlessly stand your ground, hold your own, and not allow others to dictate your mood.
- ♥ How to kick your inner critic to the curb and start appreciating yourself.

...and the list goes on.

Oh, and did I mention that you will love yourself a whole lot more by the end?

So you're probably wondering, "Who is this Trish chick, and how is she going to help me?"

First, I've been there. I'm just a few years older than you, so I totally know what's up. Second, I'm constantly traveling from state to state, getting the lowdown from middle school and high school girls about what is bothering them in their friendships. You see, I'm the founder of the nonprofit organization Sister Soldier—Stand Up for Each Other, a school assembly and empowerment program for girls. Our mission is to alleviate the pain caused by the often mean and hurtful ways that girls treat one another and also treat themselves. Pretty rad goal, right?

One of my favorite parts of an assembly is afterward, when I get to hang out with you girls and talk more in depth about your specific situations. There is never enough time to cover *all* of the important topics. This book can. It has specific advice about what to do in a number of different—yet common—situations, and it offers solutions, action steps that will make you feel way better about yourself and the junk that's bringing you down.

This is your book, your way out of the craziness and into the awesomeness that is Girl World. Cherish it like you would your phone, your celebrity crush, or those sweet new shoes you've been saving up for. It contains all the answers you will need. You'll feel more confident and secure. You'll develop strong, fulfilling friendships that lift you up rather than tear you down. And you'll discover a renewed sense of self-love.

All right, my friend. I invite you to hop aboard the love bus, because your ride is about to get wayyy better.

Peace, Love & Some Serious Upgrades,

Trish

1   YOU'RE IN—BUT ARE YOU?

We all have days that are so amazing that we want to freeze time to enjoy them—and then relive them over and over. There are also, inevitably, those horrible days that we just want to forget. A lot of what makes a day good or bad depends on the people around us, the girls in our inner-most circle.

REWIND TO ONE OF THE BEST DAYS OF SCHOOL:

You are seated at a lunch table with your friends, sharing stories, catching up on the latest news, cracking jokes… this is, hands down, the best part of the school day. There is a special kind of comfort in these friendships. You laugh hysterically at inside jokes, whisper about crushes, swap secrets, and cheer each other on. You share interests, hobbies, clothes...pretty much everything. You may even bond over insecurities or mutual dislike of certain people, which makes you feel even closer because you guys get each other. The bond between you is seemingly unbreakable. Finding this solid group of girls was definitely a highlight of your school experience. Before you know it, you're attached at the hip. You've made your friends for life.

Until that one time...

FAST-FORWARD TO ONE OF THE WORST DAYS OF SCHOOL:

You get the feeling that there's something off about the dynamics in your group. You can't quite put your finger on it, but it seems as though your friends are acting different toward you. Your mind does a quick replay of the past week, but nothing stands out. So why is everyone being weird? No one is coming out and saying what's wrong, but you definitely get the vibe that something is up.

You love your friends, though you've seen them do some not-so-nice things to other classmates, and you may have even participated at times. You know they secretly don't like Sophie and are just pretending to be her friend. You witnessed the all-out bashfest they had when Alexa was home sick the other week, and you've definitely heard their true feelings about Catherine's profile picture. You know that, at one time or another, various girls have been the target of gossip and rumors, but you have never been on the receiving end of it. So you ignore, deny, and justify your friends' point of view. You've already crowned these girls your besties for life, so you don't want to focus on their bad qualities. After all, given how close you are and all you share, their faults and shortcomings are your faults and shortcomings. Besides, they are your closest friends. They would never do anything to hurt you.

But those whispers and the occasional dirty looks are making you feel excluded. And it's happening more and more frequently. You can see the signs...

Why are people giving me one-word answers?

Why did Molly's text say "Hi" and not "Hey"?

Is Katie mad at me? She totally brushed past me this morning.

That comment was a total dig at me, wasn't it?

Why is everyone quiet when I sit down?

No, this cannot be happening!

Fear. Anxiety. Nerves. Distrust. Paranoia. Betrayal.

This girl: she is in you and she is in me. We've all experienced a version of this scenario, whether it be to a greater or lesser extent. Nothing can take away the pain of feeling burned by a friend; it's real, it's raw, and it hurts.

The bad news is it happened. The good news is you will not bottom out with nowhere to turn and not a clue what to do. I wish that I could magically erase those moments for you as if they never happened, but I can't. Instead, as someone who has been in your shoes, I can give you the next best thing: real, honest, and effective advice and action steps to get out of the situation, while guiding you to see the hazard signs and reroute yourself to prevent a similar situation in the future. My hope is that you'll take this advice to heart, because if you let it, it can truly transform your relationships.

In this chapter, we will discuss what to do if your friends are talking badly about you, you feel intimidated by certain girls, or you can't fully trust your friends. We'll also address some steps you can take if you're scared of being targeted, left out, or kicked out of a group, not to mention if you feel insecure and you're worried about missing out. *You* have to put these words into action, which also means getting honest with yourself about how you've been feeling in your friendships. The last thing you would want is to go through all those bad feelings again in a new situation.

There *is* a light at the end of the tunnel. It is important to remember that when you are feeling down. And I promise you will get to that light a whole lot faster once you pull your beautiful self out of that slump and commit to making positive changes. So good-bye woe-is-me thinking and hello I-got-this attitude. Are you ready?

BEHIND ★ YOUR ★ BACK BIZ

It's gut-wrenching to discover you're being talked about behind your back—and by people you consider your friends. Whether you know it to be true or have heard rumors, the news is a blow to one's self-esteem. It's easy to lose your cool. Your heart races; you're overwhelmed by emotion. You don't know what to feel first: hurt, sadness, anger. After the initial sting comes the feeling of betrayal. *How could she do this to me?*

We want to be able to trust our friends, to tell them anything, and why shouldn't we? Friends are supposed to have your back, not go behind it. When you get the sense that they did, it feels like a big-time violation.

When you find yourself in a situation like this, your

mind runs rampant with questions: What's my next move? Do I talk to her? How do I do that? Can I ever trust her again? Will I be able to bounce back from this?

Before we get to these questions, the first thing we need to do is dust off the dictionary and get clear on the definition of a friend. You may giggle and think it's silly, but I can't tell you how many girls have skewed ideas of what a real friend is and what true friendship entails.

. . . .

Friend (noun): A person you regard with trust. A
    companion. An ally.

. . . .

That is a good foundation, but let me Trish-a-fy this definition. A friend is someone who does not talk badly about you to anyone. A friend is someone who does not make you feel insecure, left out, embarrassed, ashamed, on edge, nervous, or afraid. A friend is someone who does not act one way to you when you're alone together and then completely different in front of other people. A friend is someone who does not make you feel as if you must compete for her attention, acceptance, or approval. If you are under the impression that any of those traits are normal in friendships, then hold tight because a little mind makeover is on its way! Now that we're clear on what friendship should look like, the second step is to get honest about the dynamic you have with your friends and how they make you feel.

Getting honest with myself was, at times, very tough because I didn't want to admit that some of my best friends made me feel uncomfortable and insecure, or that I couldn't entirely trust someone I was really close to. It was much easier to pretend that everything was okay, instead of owning how I truly felt. If I owned it, that meant I was acknowledging something wasn't right. Choosing to ignore it was pretty much the equivalent of slapping myself in the face.

I remember being absent from school one day when my inner FOMO revved up. That was a hazard sign, though I didn't pay much attention to it at first. I called one of my best friends at the time, a few minutes after I knew she would be home from school, to ask her how her day was. I was eager to see if anything interesting happened at school while I was home sick.

She responded, in a tone that sounded as if she was trying to make me jealous, "School was actually the best day ever today." I wanted to kick myself for being sick. *Of course the day I'm absent, school is a big party.* But then I remembered it was *school*, not the Fourth of July.

Although my friend's comment made me feel excluded, which wasn't nice, I now realize that I was the one to blame for my anxiety. I was the one feeding the belief that if I wasn't present every single time my friends were together, they would somehow forget me, talk about me, or push me to the outskirts of the group. If I was more secure and my friendships were healthy, we wouldn't play the games that so often cause fights or tension between friends. Bon voyage, manipulation! See you later, passive-aggressiveness!

One of my biggest breakthroughs was choosing to surround myself with people I could depend on and who I knew always had my best interests at heart. After all, friendships are supposed to be based on trust. They should be built on rock, not on sand that can shift at any time.

This way of thinking completely transformed my friendships and ultimately my happiness. I started to surround myself with people who lifted me up instead of tearing me down, with people who supported me, and with whom I could be 100 percent myself. No masks. No filter. No fakeness. When situations or conversations didn't feel right, I trusted that. Even if I couldn't exactly put my finger on why the vibe was off, I knew I should listen to my gut. Your intuition is there for a reason. It's the sane, rational part of your mind that *always* has your back and is looking out for you. Don't ignore it; it's your compass.

Now let's get back to the million-dollar question: *What do you do if your friends are talking badly about you?* Right now we are not so worried about how to approach them or figuring out what to say; there is a whole chapter dedicated to handling confrontation and dialogue in a low-key, drama-free way. Instead, we're talking about making the best decision for you. What are *you* going to do moving forward? Ask yourself: *Is this person fitting the definition of a true friend and do I feel good about myself when I am around her?* If you can't respond with a resounding yes, then perhaps this question is more fitting: *Does this person act shady at times, making me feel insecure and doubt my trust in her?*

The answer may not be what you want to hear, but *be truthful.* Otherwise you'll wind up hurting a whole lot more in the long run. The key here is differentiating whether this is a habit or an exception. If talking badly behind each other's back is a recurring theme, let's not kid ourselves; it *will* happen again. I know it's difficult to admit, because when things are good with your friends, they are *really* good. Not being able to trust someone is a sure sign that the bad in the relationship will ultimately outweigh the good.

Fortunately, you can stop yourself from getting to that point. Take a long look at your friendships and decide if they deserve your all or if taking a step back is the better option. Keep in mind that the right choice may not always be the easy thing to do.

HANGING BY A THREAD

Have you ever worried about being in the hot seat with your group of friends? Did you ever experience the nerves that come with suspecting all your friends are mad at you? It's a universal fear. No one wants to be left out or kicked out of their group. Perhaps it's because we've seen it done before to someone who, once upon a time, used to be part of the in crowd. Or maybe we've witnessed our friends go from loving a girl to, one by one, deciding they weren't too fond of her anymore.

If this has happened in the past, you've seen how ugly it can get. You might, for a split second, wonder *What if this happens to me?* Imagining yourself on the receiving end of endless dirty looks, hateful comments, and the infamous silent treatment—all from people who used to be your closest friends—is definitely enough to cause fear and bring on a case of the nerves. Once this seed of insecurity is planted, it takes root in the back of your mind. You start to get the feeling that a friend is acting different, or is mad at you, or is distancing herself. When that happens, panic starts playing games with your head, causing you to perceive situations in a distorted—and often exaggerated—way.

In order to be the cool, calm, and collected babes that we truly are, the first order of business is to recognize your method of freaking out. How does your fear show itself? What is your go-to choice of panic? It could be that you analyze e v e r y t h i n g, reading *way* too much into situations. Perhaps you cling to your friends for dear life, coming off as needy or a tad possessive. Maybe your inner sweetness is programmed to operate at an all-time high and you become *overly* nice, doing extra favors and going out of your way, using your kindness as armor. Whatever your version is, don't feel bad. We *all* do it one time or another.

Once you've identified your method, the next step is to...

MAKE YOUR MOVE

When we are anxious and nervous in our friendships, we tend to freak out over small incidents, blowing them out of proportion. If we feel like we could potentially lose a friend, our minds start bugging out. In fact, in instances like this, our minds can be our own worst enemies. We start thinking of worst-case scenarios: everyone is mad at me; everyone hates me; I have no friends; my life is over.

Sound familiar? The *moment* your mind starts going on its trip, *stop*. *Don't* go there. Because if you begin this downward spiral with your thoughts, you will go into school looking for confirmation that your friends still like you, that they aren't mad at you, and that everything is normal. This reads *needy, insecure, desperate,* and *weak,* all of which you are *not*.

Some of your "friends" might enjoy the power they have over your emotions. If you look at whatever happened *as it truly is,* without inflating the situation, you will start to realize that when your mind freaks out, the incident gets bigger. However if you downplay it, the incident gets smaller.

Recognizing how your behavior changes when you feel fearful, anxious, or nervous puts you at an advantage. Whenever you notice these patterns, silently call yourself out. This enables you to return to your brilliant authenticity.

Keep your head high when you walk into school and be kind to everyone—including yourself. Don't rehash or engage in the negativity. You will appear unfazed, making a clear statement that those tricks and mind games others play won't work on you. Watch how well people respond to your vibe.

Reflecting on your feelings and shining light on your not-so-hot behaviors is the best way to learn about yourself and switch gears to make some pretty incredible improvements. Friendship is not supposed to be hard. By incorporating this advice, not only do you put more importance on having positive, effortless friendships, but you also become a better friend.

It's not always the other person's fault. Sometimes the problem is *ourselves*. For example, we could be responsible for totally hyperventilating that our best friend is mad at us because she isn't texting back immediately, when really she's just had the busiest week imaginable. Moments of insecurity happen. That is vastly different from experiencing those feelings, or similar feelings, all the time. You don't deserve to constantly have to sweat things out or worry about being one step ahead of the game. There shouldn't be a game.

There are times we may bite our tongues about how we truly feel for the sake of being friends with *those girls,* but friendship is not about settling. It's not about dismissing your feelings. Imagine having no worries, no cares, no anxieties, and feeling good, calm, happy, and uplifted. That's what it should be like when you are with your friends; that's what they should bring out in you.

INTIMIDATION NATION

Let's admit it: there are some girls who intimidate the heck out of us. They could be in our circle of friends or it could be another girl in our grade. Maybe there's more than one person. Perhaps someone sees *you* as an intimidating girl. You never know.

Some characteristics of an intimidator are: she takes on a "leader of the pack" role, often setting the tone for the group; she's hard to confront; and she might make you feel inferior. At times, she may come off as bossy, mean, or overly confident.

Some of your friends may have admitted they feel the same way you do about this person, which can be comforting. However, despite this commonality, people are still too apprehensive to stand up to her or confront her when she's in the wrong. There is a universal desire to be liked by her, to be her friend. If that is the case, it's safe to say, there's a love-hate relationship going on.

Why is it that we can stick up to certain people and not to others? Why do girls say things behind an intimidator's back that they wouldn't dare say to her face? What is it about an intimidator that makes us recoil in fear?

Let's shine the light on ourselves first. The first move is to recognize how your behavior is different toward this person than it is toward your other friends.

Are you being yourself in those interactions? If not, try to identify what changes. Maybe you don't talk as much or are overly chatty in her presence. Do you think a lot more before you speak, to make sure you don't say something that might be perceived as "weird"? Perhaps you find yourself always agreeing with what she says or telling her only what you know she wants to hear. Have you ever tried to up your "coolness" to impress her? Don't worry; we've all been guilty of this at one time or another!

This point is not to make yourself feel bad. In fact, it's the exact opposite. We want to wake up your inner amazing and regain your confidence and composure *no matter the situation.*

If you are feeling intimidated, the way to break out of this behavior is by pulling back the layers that you have built up to protect and/or defend yourself. In doing so, you'll get to know yourself better than you ever have before. You'll start to understand *why you do what you do when you do it.* Many girls, if not all girls, have been intimidated, whether they voice it or not. When you dig deep and learn how your behavior changes when you feel intimidated, you can turn down, or off, the volume of the intimidation. By becoming aware of your habits and owning your reactions, you stay in control and don't allow others to get the best of you.

The next measure is to level the playing field. Translation: *stop inflating the intimidator.* Stop giving her way more credit, power, coolness, or popularity than she has earned. Constantly viewing her in this upgraded light only feeds into her intimidating aura. You are bound to feel bad about yourself as a result. No more holding your tongue or dodging the desire to disagree with her!

I know it's gutsy to take a stand, but you should not have to walk on eggshells or question your worth around others—particularly a friend. Even if you have to remind yourself a hundred times, before you know you'll see this intimidating girl, repeat that you are *both* amazing. No one is cooler or better than the other. Once this is drilled into your mind and you put it into action, you'll start to see your hesitancies slip away. You won't waver or tiptoe anymore, my friend. And believe me, she'll pick up on that real fast.

Remember, the intimidation factor that some girls exude does *not* make them cool. It's actually *not cool*. You can't go through life intimidating people. You have a say in who you spend time with and see on a daily basis. Gravitate toward those who lift you up, who appreciate you, and who genuinely make you feel good.

Now, as we've just discussed, there are some people who have mastered the technique of intimidation and are quite aware of their effect on others. On the other hand, there are girls who truthfully don't know that they come across as intimidating. Usually underneath that bravado is a little feeling called insecurity. It can be disguised in different ways: maybe by bragging or talking loudly. Her attempt to mask her discomfort might manifest itself in behaviors that are perceived as intimidating. Instead of assuming a girl thinks she's "better than," consider that she might feel "less than." In that case, we have to revert to good old l-o-v-e. Some extra hugs and tenderness may be in order.

CONFORMITY 101

Conformity plagues school hallways. No joke. It seems like everyone's doing it. No wonder it's so easy to get sucked in! Sometimes it happens naturally, and we're not even conscious that we're doing it (like when all of a sudden we *have* to get that hot new bracelet that everyone has). Other times, we say and do things that don't sit well with us, just because the rest of our friends are doing it. Maybe you spoke badly about someone you actually don't mind. Your friends were all sharing their criticisms of her, so you felt like you had to contribute. Maybe you've had an all-out moral earthquake, where you've been pressured to do something that just didn't feel right and it left you shaken up. One thing's for sure: it's not easy to stand your ground while the rest of your friends are caving in.

By this point, I think we've all realized that friendship isn't always *bff, ily, xoxo*—although that is the way it should be! That's what growing up is about: figuring out who you are, who you want to be, and who you can call your true friends. Along the way, you'll learn some pretty invaluable lessons, like what your limits are, when to say no, and the biggie: *staying true to yourself.*

An added bonus? You have me to help you through this! I won't leave you hanging. Below, I share some sweet aha realizations to shed some light on this issue. Let's kick conformity to the curb once and for all. Ready, set, go!

Similarity doesn't guarantee permanence.

Commonalities bring people together. They don't *bind* people together. If you were to walk around a random school and observe the students, it wouldn't take long to see the resemblance among friends. They tend to dress alike, talk alike, act alike, and in many cases, look alike. It's become second nature, almost habitual, for friends to collectively gravitate toward a certain look.

The question is: Do you dare stand out? Are you willing to put the spotlight on what makes *you* unique? Or do you hide behind the identity of your group of friends?

A good indicator of conformity is to see whether you have a filter. Are you selective with the stories and the information you share with your friends? Sometimes, whether we realize it or not, we gear our conversations toward topics or opinions that we know will be unanimously accepted, while filtering out the other stuff that might come off as controversial, out there, or uncool. Perhaps you consciously held back from saying who you hung out with or what you did the other day because you know certain friends will judge you. After all, similarities are safe—differences are potentially destructive, right? Wrong! Similarity doesn't guarantee permanence. If anything, similarity guarantees boredom.

The truth is, friends shouldn't care who you hang out with or what you do in your spare time, no matter how outlandish it may be! You should be free to have outside friends and get together with girls who may not be in your tight-knit circle. It shouldn't be awkward to do so. What if you really get along well with someone who is in a completely different social circle? That's great! You're not committing a friendship crime by hanging out with different people. It doesn't matter what your other friends might think about that person. You shouldn't have to forfeit one friendship for another. If you do, expect to make other sacrifices because your friends will see the pull they have over you, and believe me, they won't stop there. A friend should be concerned about the quality of friendship between you two, that's it.

Somewhere along the way, you may have equated happiness with being accepted by a particular group of girls. You would do anything to preserve these friendships—even if it means not being true to yourself. Adapting this mind-set will cause you to make compromises and conform, but it won't make you happier.

Do something baller. Throw away (or recycle!) all the ways in which you conform, all the ways in which you hide your personality to cater to your friends' expectations, all the ways in which you are not being yourself. It's time to break free of the pressures and insecurities that are making you stuck. OMG! Liberating, right?

Your authentic self is your happiest self.

You know that girl who enters the room and all eyes turn in her direction? She has that special glow that makes others think, *Whoa! I want what she has.* Well, here's the inside scoop: She has that glow because she's happy with herself. She's comfortable in her own skin. She doesn't wear a facade or try to impress others. She stands her ground, not letting outside pressures sway her. People naturally gravitate toward her because there's nothing more refreshing then someone who is the real deal.

You may be thinking, *Well, that's great and all, but I'm scared that people won't like me if I'm my authentic self.* Can I tell you a secret? Deep down, everyone is frightened that if she reveals who she really is—flaws and all—people will run in the opposite direction. That is why we conform, because we think it's safer to blend in.

The thing is, being happy with yourself doesn't mean that you are perfect or that you are always in a good mood. Loving yourself means acknowledging your flaws and shortcomings, but instead of disguising them or pretending that they don't exist, you own them and move on. You know that happiness you crave? You will find it when you let go of the ways in which you conform to others' expectations and instead recognize that your truest self is pretty spectacular. No person, no group of friends, no possessions, no status, *nothing* will give you a buzz like when you're living authentically.

What's ironic is we think that by saying and doing things that go along with the groove of our group, we are more likely to retain our friends. It's actually the opposite. The more you stay true to yourself, the more friends you will have. People are attracted to girls who are genuine; people want to be around girls who are authentic. Being your true self transforms you into a magnet, and you'll attract a whole lot of greatness into your life.

If you truly want to be happy, do more of what you love, say how you really feel, spend time with people who love you for you, and don't be afraid to say no. There are people who will adore the person you truly are, differences and all.

2 THE OUTSIDE LOOKING IN

Now that we've tackled some common friend issues, let's talk about what happens when you're struggling to make friends to begin with. Have you ever felt like you don't fit in when all you want is to belong? If so, you're not the only one. We've all been there. *Many* girls (and guys) have difficulty making friends; there is nothing wrong with you.

We care a lot about what other people think of us, and it can be challenging when we don't feel accepted. You are spectacular, and there *are* ways to pull yourself into a more positive, enjoyable place. By getting honest about how you feel, you can learn to turn those negative feelings around and improve your overall happiness.

This chapter is for anyone who has ever felt as if she had no one by her side, no friends to fall back on. Whether you've felt this way for a long time or it's been brought on by a recent situation, we will discuss what to do when you feel like you have few, if any, friends; don't quite fit in; feel left out or excluded; or used to be in a group but all your friends have turned against you.

Believe me. I know how difficult this can be. Remember: there are other people encountering the same hurdles. I'm here to share some comfort, healing, and guidance. Know that I have your back!

ODD GIRL OUT

Weird. Weird is a word I wish never existed. I can't tell you how many times I've heard girls say, "She's so weird." Nine out of ten times (or more like 9.99 times!), "weird" is used in a negative and hurtful way to exclude others. No one wants to feel like a total freak or a straight-up alien from another planet.

Feeling as if you are missing the piece to the puzzle that every other girl seems to have is one of the *hardest* internal battles to combat. When you're in that space and lower than low, it's easy to think: *What's wrong with me?* Hang tight. By the end of this chapter, we are going to slingshot that thought right out of your mind and refocus on what's *right*.

If you feel like you are lacking in the friends department (and I've been there), it's understandable that your self-esteem and confidence levels may be well below where they should be. Every single day at school, one is swarmed by cliques roaming the hallways together, sitting and laughing together, doing homework together. In other words, it can feel like a constant reminder that you don't quite fit in.

This may seem foreign to some girls, and if you are one of them, I can't stress enough how important it is to consider how others might feel. We see people hanging solo all the time and brush it off, thinking, *Oh that's just who they are. They like being alone.* Do they? We forget that many of our peers want the same things we want. Acceptance and friendship rank high on that list.

One of the most important lessons I learned, if not *the* most important lesson, is: you cannot shape your identity and self-worth by how many friends you have or how others feel about you. For too long, I searched for validation from other people, instead of validating myself. I needed others to confirm that I was well liked, cool enough, good enough, and pretty enough. When I thought that people liked me, I liked myself more. When I saw people draw back, I drew back on myself. The thing is…that's a really shaky surface to be standing on.

Instead of letting time go by and waiting for others to make you feel good about yourself, why not feel good about yourself *now*? Don't sit idly, thinking that there's nothing you can do about how you feel and wishing you could be someone else. The only thing you need to change is that thought.

So how do you do that? The first order of business is to remember that *you* can build yourself up. You are in charge of the whole construction process and what the end result will be. Maybe it's time for some renovation! Demolish the bad stuff. Get rid of the hazardous materials. Start from the ground up, working slowly and carefully to assemble a strong foundation. What are the qualities that make you special? Are you smart? Funny? Kind? Have a talent for playing a sport or an instrument or some other hobby? Think of all of the great aspects that make you *you*, and build a foundation of self-worth that is so sturdy and so reliable that *no one else*, I repeat, *no one else*, will be able to shake you. Because…

Truth #1: There are always going to be people who give you a hard time, no matter what.

The haters will always hate. Why let them have a say in how you view yourself? Your self-image and self-worth depend on what you think of you, not what others think of you.

Take a quick mental scan of the people in your life. Are there any uneasy feelings that come to mind when you think of certain people? Is there anyone who makes you feel uncomfortable rather than positive and secure? If so, that is a flashing red light telling you to keep your distance. Pay attention to it. That relationship is not building you up.

Next, pause to listen to the messages that are playing on repeat in your mind. Are they inspiring you, or are they saying you're not pretty enough or smart enough? If they are weighing you down, I want you to ask yourself, says who? Where is that sentiment coming from? If it's another person, you have to realize that no one gave them the power to decide who is good enough and who is not. If you are the one saying those things, you've just identified the culprit. And guess what? Now you have the chance to change that message. That damaging thought is no longer welcome. Choose a different thought, a more loving and real one: I am good enough. I am pretty enough. I am smart enough.

After you've done all this work on your foundation, you're not about to let it crumble again, right? Stay firm in your commitment to take care of yourself. Don't let anyone take away your shine. Dirty looks, hurtful comments, feelings of unworthiness and isolation—show them the door. Don't let them get inside your head and camp out. Because...

Truth #2: You are not any of the negative things that other people call you.

Quite the contrary, you are someone who is so special, so talented, and so deserving. There is no one else in the world quite like you.

That is why we cannot let the thoughts and actions of others diminish our potential to be great. Sometimes staying small almost feels safer than playing it big. If you're a behind-the-scenes kind of gal who doesn't like the spotlight, that is totally okay. When we feel inadequate or invisible based on how our peers view us, we tend to shrink and hide—and that's a problem. Thoughts of not being good enough can be paralyzing, preventing us from dreaming big. What if we were to bust through that wall, dream big, and fearlessly go after what we want? Be honest: Does that intimidate you?

Without a doubt, your mind is INCREDIBLY POWERFUL. It has the ability to make you feel like you are this small or THIS BIG. But of course, it depends on what you tell yourself, what you choose to believe. When you feel like an outsider, all those funky thoughts get in your head and bring you down. It can be extremely challenging to rise up when the world seems to be telling you to sit down.

You know what? No one benefits if you play small. I don't care if you have zero friends, one friend, or fifty friends; you are talented and unique and have your own gifts to share with the world. Mind over matter, girls. Play big.

ODD GIRL OUT 2 (THE SEQUEL)

There's another type of being singled out that happens quite often. Rather than being an outcast because a girl is "different" than everyone else, this girl had a group of friends who, for some reason or another, turned against her.

It's like living in a nightmare. One day you're surrounded by people you think are your really good friends, and then the next day you're on the outside looking in. It occurred so quickly, you got whiplash! Often there are no warning signs, so it makes it harder to process. *Is this real life? Is this actually happening?* Two seconds ago these girls were your BFFs and now they're your arch nemeses. Wait—what? Hold up!

A deep-rooted sense of betrayal comes to mind. Friends can turn into frenemies overnight, and girls are left blindsided. It's rarely just one person who turns her back; everyone from the group usually hops on board the hate train. Often there's no rhyme or reason for why they do so. Perhaps it's out of boredom and the need for entertainment. The circle of friends may have crafted excuses for what the girl might have done wrong, but rarely does anyone deserve total and complete alienation.

Now our girl's forced to navigate the hallways by herself and make all new friends (that is, unless her ex-besties corrupt other people's opinions). How can she make new friends without being fearful and distrusting?

The reason I understand this girl and what she is going through is because *I was that girl*. It happened to me.

I was in seventh grade when all my friends got mad at me on the same day, at the same time, and I felt like a deer in headlights. I had no clue why it was happening. And when it persisted, that year became the most difficult year of my life. It had an impact on who I was and the trust I had for others for quite some time. Years have passed and all is forgiven, but my heart still hurts whenever I think back on it. I don't know if that will ever go away. But it's a part of me, part of my story, and if I can use that experience to help someone else avoid a similar situation, it was well worth it.

You *do* have the power to get through an incident like this. You are not hopeless or helpless. The power lies in how you *perceive* your surroundings and how you are *acting* within them. Instead of letting the situation control your thoughts and feelings, *you* must take hold of the reins. Shifting your thoughts to include more positive messages is a sure way to improve the situation. You can't bank on your "friends" coming around and for your relationships to magically get better. If you want to feel better, gain confidence, and be happier, you have to make a conscious effort to do so. Here's what you can do…

MAKE YOUR MOVE

Make time in your schedule, *every single day*, to boost your mood. Mood-booster time cancels out the moping-around-your-house-in-sweats-listening-to-a-depressing-song-on-repeat time. I am going to be tough on you for this step because it *works!* You, my friend, are *strong*.

Write a list of all the things that you enjoy. What makes you smile and brightens your day? Refer to this list whenever you are feeling down. You cannot control what others do and say, but you *can* control how you react and if you let it affect you. Before a situation gets the best of you, pull out this list and think of one of the happy moments there or complete one of the activities you wrote down.

If you dwell in a low space for a long time, you can start to wallow in those feelings. But if you decide to take action and do something to change that, *you* have power over your life, your feelings, your vibes, your mood. Do *not* let others dictate *your* state of mind. Don't put *your happiness* in the hands of someone else!

Next, seek out a new community. Look for people whose company you genuinely enjoy and with whom you can see yourself forming friendships. Don't limit yourself to just your school district. Perhaps you can join an out-of-school sports league or take some sort of arts or dance class. Maybe you volunteer for an organization that interests you or apply for a part-time job where you'll meet people who are of a similar age.

Never *stop* making friends. I know some of you may be thinking that you're set for life with your BFF soul sistas, but things happen. Life throws curveballs, and what bad can come from having different groups of supporting, loving friends in your life?

It's easier to meet people when you're doing it casually, rather than desperately searching for new friends. If you consistently make one or two steps to surround yourself with new people, than you're really looking out for you!

Having different groups of friends helps a *ton* when there are conflicts and arguments in your crowd. You won't feel as though your *whole world just ended*. Life doesn't become a soap opera, maybe just a dramatic scene. You will not feel stranded or deserted, and you'll be able to rely on—and learn from—other people, not just one tight-knit group.

Also, having several different circles of friends provides a basis for comparison. You'll be able to recognize the friends who are good to you and good for you, rather than those who weren't such good friends after all. When you have a steady stream of people in your life, you'll be able to recognize the qualities of great friendships and start to weed out the bad ones from the good.

Last but not least, let's revisit an old saying that carries a lot of truth—*quality over quantity*. Friendship is *all about* quality. If you are ever the odd girl out, I want you to remember that, in the end, it doesn't matter how many friends you have. This is a common misconception. All too often a busy social calendar or an increasing number of friends on social media boosts our self-esteem and confidence. If you have *one* great, true friend, you're set for life. Don't think you are lacking a thing, because really, you are *so lucky*. One phenomenal friendship is far more fulfilling than twenty superficial friendships. One amazing friend will not isolate and turn others against you.

Big groups can be overwhelming and intimidating, so not everyone wants to be part of a large friendship circle. I personally find that being surrounded by large groups can feel like sensory overload with eighty-five different conversations going on all at once. When you're constantly in a group with a lot of people, it prevents you from *really* getting to know each person as an individual and keeping up with the important things that are happening in their lives. There's something to be said about having several smaller groups of friends whose friendships were formed for different reasons.

If you find yourself bumming out and feeling like you don't have enough friends, I want you to stop, drop (if so desired), and scream: quality over quantity!

PARTY FOR ONE

So you never got the invite to the big party… This happens to *every single girl*—actually, *every single person*—at one point or another. Yes, it even happens to the girls we think of as "perfect," whose biggest problems, to us at least, seem to be that they are so popular.

Feeling excluded because you weren't invited somewhere is probably the most common complaint that I hear about from girls. No one wants to be left out. When we find we didn't make the guest list, our mood goes from high to low at record speed. We can't help but take it personally and want to open the floodgates to anger, hurt, and sadness. Cue the emotions—it's about to be a long night...

Feelings of disapproval or unhappiness with who we are quickly begin to surface. We put ourselves under a micro-scope and start directing the questions inward. *Why me? Why wasn't I invited? What's wrong with me?* While you're completely entitled to feel sad (in fact, I encourage you to be real with those feelings so they are validated), our biggest mistake is thinking that we are somehow not good enough to be invited.

Don't kick yourself when you're already down. If that happens, you have my full support to talk back to those inner thoughts. Politely ask them to leave. This is not the time to feel bad about yourself. This is the time to turn up the self-love. Let's take a look at where things could have gone wrong. Before we decide it was an evil, malicious plot (don't worry, we will get to that possibility), let's take a step back and examine our expectations.

First, we can't realistically expect that when we become friends with someone, we will be invited to *every* event in their life. We are definitely not going to be included every single time. I know it's tough love, but you can't take it personally.

Second, maybe we assume that we're closer to a certain friend than we actually are. If that could be true for you, just keep hanging out and getting to know those friends better. The strongest friendships are built over time.

There are other possibilities too. Maybe we said no to a similar event in the past and our friends assume we don't enjoy certain activities or are too busy. Maybe we recently got into a tiff with someone and they need a little bit more time to cool down and move forward. Or maybe we aren't aware that other girls have a tradition or activities that they are used to doing together or are looking to get to know one another better themselves.

After we've taken into account that you may have been expecting too much or are being extra sensitive, perhaps we *can* determine that there was an ulterior motive for purposely excluding you. If that's the case, it's 100 percent okay to be upset about it. That is a tough pill to swallow, especially when your closest friends are the ones responsible. By this point, that voice on your inner intercom system should be warning you loud and clear that these girls may not be acting like true friends. Well, listen up, because your inner voice is right! Remember the definition of what it is to be a friend. Deliberately excluding someone with the intention of causing pain is not cool. It's not something that real friends do.

When I said you should be dialing up the self-love, I

meant it! At times like this, you can do one of two things: you can close your door, turn off the lights, get into bed, and sulk *or* (and this option is way more fun) you can throw a party for one. That's right: throw a party for you!

Whether you plunge headfirst into your favorite dessert, have a wild dance party in your room, or settle in to watch your favorite movie that you've seen a hundred times but never get sick of, make sure that you do something that you absolutely LOVE. It may sound silly, but, believe me, a party for one is far more fun than chillin' next to your tissue box. Whatever you choose to do, relax, have fun, and kick it with your cool self.

For the grand finale, let me introduce you to what I like to call a "serious love throw-down." Sounds intense, right? It is. Up your self-love game like never before. It's the only way to turn those funky feelings into something more useful. Here's how:

Put Post-its with loving comments in places that you look often. For example: *Hey, self, you are amazing!* Have fun with it! Leave them in your bedroom, bathroom, on your laptop, or even use them as bookmarks to remind you that you are special.

Hug yourself. I know it may sound silly, but you should get in the habit of showing yourself some much-deserved love! It feels good to hug yourself. It's a way of telling yourself, *I'm proud of you, I have your back, I love you, and you're doing a great job.*

Commit to loving yourself and being compassionate

toward yourself in the morning, during the day, and at night. Be good to yourself on your good days and on your bad days. Love yourself when you fail and when you succeed. Love yourself when you're the life of the party and when you're riding solo. Don't just encourage yourself when everything's going right, because the top of one mountain often leads down to the bottom of another. How *you treat you* sets the stage for how *others treat you*. Never forget that.

One last thing—it would be really admirable if you could take your experience of being left out and learn from it. Become the Invitation Queen. Be inclusive. Invite everyone. If you're still on somewhat good terms with the people who left you out, maybe consider extending an invitation to them too. It may even help mend your friendship. I know that can be a *really hard* thing to do, but I'm just throwing it out there. You'll look back and think, *Wow, that was really cool of me*. Because being kind truly is.

3 A CHAPTER YOU COME BACK TO

School is a place where lots of laughs are shared and friendships and memories are made. However, by the time graduation rolls around, most of us are ready to leave middle school or high school behind. No matter how much we want to move on to bigger and better things, we can't just throw away our experiences as if they never happened. You might think that on the day you are handed your fancy diploma, you can run for the hills and never look back. You've graduated! Case closed! *Hasta la vista!* I hate to be the bearer of bad news, but that's not quite what happens.

You will come back to this chapter in your life time and time again. When you meet new people, you'll be asked about where you grew up and went to school and what your friends were like. So if we were bullied, we'll look back with sadness, remembering the people who made it difficult for us. If we were unkind to people, we have to relive that too. In time, the guilt and remorse hits us.

The present is significant. The person we are now *is* shaping who we will become. One moment leads to the next. Everything is connected. *Really.* You have the ability to help shape your experiences, so take charge of the moment!

In this chapter, you'll find the most valuable lessons that I learned from my time at school. They are ideals that I always come back to—and some of my top, go-to advice that I give girls at my assemblies. You may have heard some of these ideas before, which just goes to show how golden they are.

It's like a mini-toolbox! Use these concepts to fix problems or prevent an accident. (Really *use* them!) Make changes *now* and be proud of the person you are. Don't look back at your school years with guilt or sadness, wishing you could have done things differently. You can write your now and be the person you want to be. Make this the best chapter of your life!

WORD.

Okay, you want the truth? Everything you say is *extremely* powerful. Every remark, every comment, every statement carries a charge. And it's either positive or negative. How are you using this power? Are you lifting others up or bringing others down?

What's cool and scary at the same time is that we all have a pretty big vocabulary. There's definitely no shortage of insults. There is a whole lot of praise we could be giving out too, yet, for some reason, we are more selective with that. In our society, it's almost become second nature to judge and criticize others, either outwardly or in our heads. We do it so frequently that we rarely stop and think about what we are saying; we just say it. It's as if we are numb to the meaning behind the words we speak.

Then there are the labels. There's a tendency to categorize others: *a popular girl, a nerd, a jock, a loner, a scholar, an athlete, a theater girl, a goth, a prep...* The thing is, labeling is based on stereotypes, and stereotypes have a bad rep for a reason.

Why do we throw around labels left and right like they don't mean anything? We do it to simplify. Instead of making the effort to get to know the ins and outs of a person, what their real personality is like, what their interests and hobbies are, we figure out what mold she best fits into, and we mentally put a label on her. Every person is far more complex and dynamic than that. You are more than just a stereotype, and so are the people around you. A girl is not simply an athlete. That might be *one* aspect of her personality, but her other skills and attributes may be vastly different than what you might expect of a typical athlete. There's a quote I once read that says, "Labels are for containers, not people." I strongly agree.

These labels, along with the hurtful names and comments,

get their power because of the long-lasting impact that they have on others. When we are going through school, constantly surrounded by our peers, it's easy to lose sight of the meaning behind our insults because of the frequency with which we both hear *and* say them. But horrible, unkind words stick with people for *years,* as they try to prove to themselves that they aren't the names they've been called.

It's not just what someone labels them; it's the emotions that came with it. That is why you remember for so long. An intense feeling of pain is hard to forget. I know that I can recall, like it was yesterday, the hurtful comments that my "friends" said to me. Ask your parents. Do they remember an upsetting comment from when they were your age? I bet they do!

You can't control what other people say, but you can control the impact and longevity of *your* words. Which brings us to our first lesson…

LESSON #1: BE ACCOUNTABLE FOR WHAT YOU SAY (A.K.A. OWN YOUR WORDS)

Basically, every single thing that you say, whether it comes from your mouth, your cell phone, or your computer, belongs to you. Take responsibility for it. Ask yourself: Whatever I say behind someone's back, would I say it to his or her face? Whatever tone I use in my text messages, would I use the same tone in person? Whatever gossip I am putting out there, am I willing to own it?

Whoever made up that saying, "If you don't have

anything nice to say, don't say anything at all," was right on the money. If everyone did this, there would be a lot (emphasis on the *a lot*) less headaches and bad feelings. Bon voyage, 99 percent of girl problems!

This includes hearsay, the silent killer. "I *heard* you said that. I *heard* you were talking behind my back." This kind of talk is a recipe for disaster.

Remember that game Telephone that we played back when we were little tater tots? By the time a message went through the entire class, it was totally different from what the first person said. That is because everybody puts a spin on things. People translate and communicate messages differently.

Whenever you want to approach a friend about something that you heard, wait until you know *exactly* what was said. Don't just speculate. Even if you heard something from a trusty source, don't assume it to be the full truth. People do things for excitement, for shock value, for the thrill of the drama. Unless you have proof, everything else is just hearsay. Honestly, it's a cop-out. That is why you have to be account-able for what you say and if you do talk badly about someone behind their back (even those of us with the best of intentions do so at some point or another), you should be comfortable enough with what you put out there to say it to her face.

UNLIMITED

We are all guilty of limiting ourselves. We limit who we associate with and how much we think others will like us. We limit our goals and our dreams. We also limit our self-worth and self-praise. And this business happens *way more* than you might realize. Many of us have hundreds, even thousands of limiting thoughts a day. Maybe they are directed inward: *I can't do that, I'm not good enough (cool enough, athletic enough, artistic enough), I won't make that team, I can't get that part.* Or perhaps we project those limitations outward, onto our environment: we only want to be a part of one group of friends, or we only want to play one position on a sports team or get one specific role in the play.

Thinking in terms of limits and that there are only a few spots to go around creates a competitive mentality that is the root of many problems. It sets us up to think that we can't possibly get all of the things that we need in order to be happy. While there is validity to our feelings (it's totally okay to be bummed out if we don't achieve a goal we've been working toward), sometimes—whether we realize it or not—we take our disappointment out on others.

For example, we get jealous when the person we like likes someone else. We get upset when another girl gets the part in the play we were dying for. We get angry when our friends get invited to that party we wanted to go to. When we really dig deep, our limiting beliefs and the tight restrictions we place on what would make us happy are often the culprit behind long-standing resentments, hatreds, and fights with other girls.

Although school is definitely an important chapter in your

life, it is not your whole life. You will have many adventures beyond school's hallways. Your life will be rich, exciting, full, and dynamic. You'll go on to meet so many people from so many different places. You'll meet friends of friends. Maybe you'll travel. You'll explore different activities and interests that you might not have even known you liked.

If you didn't make one team, try out for a different one. If you can't sit at one table, sit at another with people who welcome you. Getting asked to that *one* dance by that *one* person is not the be-all and end-all. You'll have much more fun if you are open to new experiences. Trust me.

The problem with having limiting thoughts is that we are setting ourselves up to be let down. We literally *limit* the goodness that can come into our lives by being so selective in what we want. Things have to go *this way*. We have to get *just that one thing*. If we don't, we're crushed. We try so hard to be seen, to be heard, to be the best, to get the most. But the truth is there *is* more than enough. There are more than enough clubs to get involved in; there are more than enough sports teams to join; there are more than enough people to be friends with; there are more than enough chairs to sit in. There *is* room for everyone. If you find that's not the case, start a new club or intramural team or invite new classmates to join you at lunch.

It's time to change those limited thoughts to **un**limited ones. No more narrow, my-way-or-the-highway thinking. Go bigger, extend wider, think in abundance. And most important…

LESSON #2: DON'T SET LIMITS
ON YOUR HAPPINESS

Example: that one group of friends + one crush + one sports team = *happy me*.

Instead of thinking in terms of limitations, start thinking in terms of possibilities. Okay, so you don't make the cheerleading team. Now what? Check what other teams are still having tryouts, what clubs you could become a member of. Maybe you trade cheerleading for gymnastics. Maybe if you don't get a role in the play, you help design the costumes. It may not be your first choice, but having options keeps you involved—and open to new kinds of fun. You'll take that bummed-out feeling and turn it right around. And when you can do something good in a bad situation, that makes you unbelievably awesome.

Also, how do you know you don't like something unless you try? We bank on x, y, and z happening because we have positive associations with it. It pairs up well with our identity or at least what we want our identity to be. When things don't work out in our favor, we take it really personally because it's more than just being, say, a member on a team. It's about being *perceived* as a part of something more. Even if you have negative associations with option #2, 3, or 4, even if you think, *I would never do that; I wouldn't be caught dead doing that*, go with it, give it a try. When you broaden your horizon, you are opening yourself up to a lot more joy and a lot more fun, and a lot more friends come rollin' on in. Who knows? Maybe you'll be signing up to do it again next year. At the very least, you went outside your comfort zone, you took a leap of faith, you became more well-rounded, you tried out something new, and you did something about your disappointment… and that's pretty cool.

DRAMA OVERLOAD

There's no lack of drama in school, especially among girls. It's *always* there. There is always *something* going on. Before we know it, we become swept into its chaos. We fall into the trap and start engaging in drama every day. Either we are directly involved in a situation, or we are gossiping about one from the sidelines. It's as if we can't survive without it. What would we talk about? (Hint: *lots!*)

When a seed is planted, it grows. The more people who add their take on a situation, the more manipulated, exaggerated, and taken out of context the situation becomes. There's no such thing as a healthy dose of drama. Once the drama heats up, it's hard to put out the fire.

Let's admit it: it's easy to gossip about someone else. There's always something we can pick apart or find fault in. We share a comment and our friend adds hers, and then someone else at the table inserts their opinion. Before we know it, we just spent twenty minutes talking about how wrong someone is. Those twenty minutes are wasted. We could have been lifting someone up instead of tearing them apart, or laughing instead of gossiping.

Some of us may think it's just meaningless gossip, but if it's so meaningless, then why are we talking about it? We've gotten in this habit of obsessing over insignificant things that others do. *She did this. She said what?!* We forget that no one is perfect. It's like no one is allowed to be human anymore, no one is allowed to make mistakes. It almost feels as though we are living under a microscope where people are waiting for us to slip up so they can talk about it.

Engaging in this insignificant drama has more of an effect than we think. Drama builds upon drama. A little gossip here and there tends to segue into something bigger. Another person listening tells someone else, the girl we were talking about finds out, a fight starts, and then there's full-blown drama fever!

How do we dial the drama back a notch so we don't hit an overload? That's where the next lesson can help us:

LESSON #3: DIFFERENTIATE BETWEEN THE STUFF THAT MATTERS (AND THE STUFF YOU CAN LET GO)

In other words: don't sweat the small stuff. Don't get sucked into the drama. At times, there's so much of it that it starts to feel like the norm, and the more we engage in it, the harder it is to detach. Sometimes it can feel exciting to be part of it—almost a little addictive. But mostly the drama makes us start trippin' over insignificant matters. We have mini-meltdowns. We flip out over unimportant stuff. And we fly off the handle at the slightest remark.

Getting hung up on drama can literally make you sick. I'm not trying to be dramatic (pun intended), but it really can. When the drama is headed in our direction, we get stressed out, anxious, and nervous. We start feeling paranoid that everyone's talking about us or that someone is trying to sabotage us. Perhaps we start second-guessing our true friends. We pay *extra* close attention to the signs. *How are they treating us? Are they acting different? Did she look at me strangely? Did she just whisper something?* We tune into even the slightest of clues that may confirm those thoughts that are bugging out in our minds. And all that is *no good*. We cannot put our energy into this negativity because it only breeds more of it.

The same thing happens when we're gossiping about others. There is this *need* to be involved in the craziness, but then it doesn't stop! We get in the habit of talking about everyone—the people we don't like and even the people who are our friends—and none of that is cool. We want to feel good about ourselves, we want to feel proud of ourselves, and that's not easy when we're engaging in drama and gossip.

I'm all for girls taking a drama-free pledge, but that just doesn't seem realistic. Life hands you curveballs and drama is inevitable. Take a step back. What is important and what can you let go of? You can control how much drama you let into your world. You don't have to contribute or engage in it. And whenever you're tempted, silently say to yourself: "Their drama is *not mine* to deal with."

Remember, friendships can still be made when you're not bonding over mutual dislikes or sharing negative opinions about others. There is no need to get excitement or entertainment out of the next new OMG drama moment. Life is full of good kinds of excitement! In the end, when you decide to not be involved, you will feel better about yourself, you will feel better about your time in school, and you'll look back feeling proud of yourself because of how you treated others.

THE S WORD

I'm going to jump right into this next lesson. It has to do with that oh-so-dreaded S word. *Sorry.* Every single person, no matter how kind or nice or innocent she is, has done something that has hurt someone else. It's nothing to be ashamed of, because how can we grow into the best versions of ourselves if we don't learn from our mistakes? We've *all* done something wrong that we later regretted... but we don't *always* apologize.

In fact, I'm sure we can all think back to an incident from our past that wasn't resolved properly, that didn't end with an "I'm sorry," and that still causes a pit in our stomachs whenever we think about it. Unresolved issues don't get better no matter how much time passes. They always stay just like that: *unresolved*. The only way to change that is with an apology. That is why...

LESSON #4: IT'S NEVER TOO LATE TO SAY "I'M SORRY"

It's not always easy to admit when we've messed up or to

take the proper steps to remedy it. It's gutsy to own our mistakes. It takes courage to apologize. None of us are perfect. An apology says, *I'm human, I mess up, but I'm also real and I'm honest, and I am sorry.* Someone who apologizes for her wrongdoings respects herself enough to not want to carry that guilt, and hopefully the apology also relieves the person who was wronged from any ill feelings as well. That is a commendable trait.

There are plenty of times when we don't want to apologize because the person we hurt has hurt us in the past, but their wrong doesn't make our wrong any less wrong. (Whoa, say that five times fast!) We can't control what others do, but we control our actions and words. If we did do something that we aren't feeling great about, we should mend it with an apology.

If you even have an inkling or small voice that's encouraging you to say sorry, listen. An apology will put the situation to rest and make you feel better.

It is *never* too late to say "I'm sorry." It doesn't matter if it's been a week, a month, a year, five years, or longer. Granted, it might feel a little awkward getting in touch with someone after that much time has passed, but extending an apology is worth the awkwardness. No one wants to hurt. If you know you hurt someone, why not give the both of you the opportunity to heal? After all, time might ease some of the sadness, but it doesn't take away the pain of the memory.

Think about someone who has hurt you. What would it

feel like to receive an apology from them? Wouldn't it feel good? Wouldn't you feel lighter? Happier? Why not share those good feelings with someone you wronged in the past?

If she accepts your apology with an open heart, that's amazing! You'll both be able to replace those negative feelings with positive ones and move on. If for some reason the apology is *not* well received (which would be less likely, because no one likes to hang on to old conflicts), you will still know that you did the right thing. And *you* will feel better.

It's time to clear the slate. And that's a win-win situation for everyone!

MAKE YOUR MOVE

Our days are stuffed to the max with school, sports, clubs, plans, and homework, and we rarely have ten seconds to take a step back and reflect. The downside of keeping up with this hustle and bustle is that we don't pause to look at how we interact with others and with ourselves unless something is wrong. But what if you were more aware of your behaviors and could proactively make them better, more positive?

Well, this is the time to do that. This exercise will help you see how you are treating other people—and yourself. Be honest as you take the quiz. You don't have to share your answers with anyone if you don't want to. That is why it's so important to be upfront and truthful. Sugarcoating your answers does not help anyone, especially you. We all have some work to do, so let's get the ball rolling!

1. Have you ever discovered a friend was talking about you behind your back?

   Yes   No

2. Have you ever talked badly about a friend behind her back?

   Yes   No

3. Have you ever denied something that you said about another girl?

   Yes   No

4. When a girl walks into the room, is your immediate reaction to judge, rather than compliment her?

   Yes   No

5. Do you label others?

   Yes   No

6. Have you ever been mislabeled?

   Yes   No

7. Have you ever been called a hurtful name?

   Yes   No

8. Have you ever called someone a name that you
   later regretted?
   Yes   No

9. Have you ever approached a friend about
   something that you "heard"?
   Yes   No

10. Do you place limits on what you are capable
    of/deserve?
    Yes   No

11. Do you place limits on what you want/need to
    be happy?
    Yes   No

12. Do you have a backup plan in case those goals
    are not met?
    Yes   No

13. Do you sweat the small stuff, making a bigger
    deal about the details than is necessary?
    Yes   No

14. When you get together with your friends, do
    you gossip about other girls?
    Yes   No

15. Are you waiting/hoping for someone to apolo-
    gize for something she did or said that really
    hurt you?

    Yes   *No*

16. Is there something you might have done in the
    past that you feel badly about but still haven't
    apologized for?

    Yes   *No*

17. Are you amazing?

    Yes   *No*

(Hint: the answer to that last one is yes)

If you answered these questions candidly, you probably noticed a few areas that could use some attention. Don't
worry—everyone has room to improve themselves and their
interactions with others! Instead of welcoming any bad feelings
that might have popped up during the quiz, I want you to
be proud of yourself for acknowledging behaviors that could
benefit from a little change. Now that you see where you
can improve, you can take the initiative to do so. And that
will ultimately make you feel better about yourself and your
friends and, overall, make you feel more fulfilled and content.

» Identify: Reread your answers. What theme or

issue is creating the most stress in your life? That's usually the best place to start making changes!

» **Evaluate:** How is your behavior contributing to the situation?

» **Strategize a solution:** How will you respond to create a different, more positive outcome? Will you disengage? Bring a positive attitude to help shift the dynamic? Generate some specific ideas.

» **Act:** Now go out and do it!

THE UGLY TRUTH

Bullying is an epidemic. There are no ifs, ands, or buts about it. Bullying is a widespread, daily crisis affecting millions of young people from every part of the world. One in six American schoolchildren report being bullied two to three times a month or more, with *many* incidents lasting for more than a year.[1] One hundred sixty thousand kids stay home from school *every* day because they are afraid of being bullied.[2] No matter how different people may appear to be, *everyone* has a bullying story, whether they were the victim, the bully, or a witness. Bullying transcends any sort of barrier. It doesn't only affect a few races or ethnicities. It doesn't just target certain geographic locations or those of a particular economic status. There are bullies *everywhere*, and they use abuse, whether emotional, verbal, physical, or even

. . . .

1. Olweus Bullying Prevention Program
2. Center for Disease Control and Prevention

cyber, to dominate others. Bullies thrive on making their victims feel powerless and inferior.

The only way we can fix the problem of bullying is to recognize that there *is* a problem and to address our contribution to it. In this chapter, we'll take a deeper look into the harmful ways that us girls interact and communicate with one another. We're also going to fast-forward to how this will affect our future selves if we stay stuck in these toxic, hurtful patterns. Don't worry—once we get past this tough stuff, we'll be on a nonstop, one-way ride to paradise. Better pack your shades, because it's gonna be bright.

BULLYING (OVERT VS. COVERT)

Before you say, "Wait, Trish, I don't *really* get bullied. I'm going to flip to the next chapter," I want you to understand what I mean when I use the word *bullied*. Yes, there are those severe forms of bullying that are extremely aggressive and alarming. This includes physically harming, verbally assaulting, threatening, and/or ganging up on someone—in other words, the **overt** types of bullying. It is absolutely crucial that these behaviors are addressed and that people take action and intervene because *no one* should *ever* be treated this way. All too often, however, these extreme, glaring instances of bullying are where the attention starts and stops.

What about the more subtle forms of bullying that easily go unnoticed by parents, teachers, and sometimes other friends, yet leave deep, lasting emotional scars? This is the

covert side to bullying and it can include: teasing, intimidating, embarrassing, insulting, gossiping, spreading rumors, name-calling, eye rolling, manipulating, excluding, and giving the silent treatment. Does that sound familiar, ladies?

These types of behaviors wreak *havoc* in Girl World, creating chaos left and right. Covert forms of bullying have become so common in female relationships that they are often referred to as *relational aggression.* Relational aggression is any act that is intended to harm others through deliberate manipulation of their social standing and relationships. Particularly during our teenage years, our friendships and social status feel incredibly important to us. They tend to be part of how we define ourselves to others. The way bullies are going to bring someone down, then, is to go after what is most important to a girl. That typically includes turning others against her, leaving her out of social activities, humiliating her, and a whole host of other examples. *Relational* aggression damages *relationships.* And relational aggression is *bullying.*

Whoa, are girls really that vicious? Maybe not on the surface, but let's take a deeper look.

According to ConfidenceCoalition.org, *a girl is bullied every seven minutes.* We've adapted what bullying expert Rachel Simmons calls a "hidden culture of aggression in girls." It's the nasty comments, the whispers, the insults said under one's breath, the sarcasm, the body language, the silent treatment, the power complex of who is superior/who is inferior, the cliques and alliances to certain groups, the passive-aggressiveness. And who can forget the judgments?

They are practically automatic. Within .05 seconds of meeting someone, we've already got them pegged...

> She's too thin, she's not thin enough, she's stupid, she's a nerd.

> She's ugly, her nose it too big, her chest is so flat.

> She's spoiled, she's trashy, she has no friends, she's fake, she's a slut, she's a tomboy, she's so conceited, she's a freak.

Yeah...girls can be mean.

By now you can see that bullying is WAY more common than you might have thought. When I talk about bullying, it includes the entire spectrum of negative behaviors, the obvious, overt forms and the sly, covert forms, because they both have significant, harmful effects. The methods of attack may vary, but the motive stays the same: to hurt someone.

So ask yourself: Have you been bullied? And perhaps more important: Have you been a bully?

THE EFFECTS

We all enter the world as beautiful, innocent individuals who want the same thing: to be happy and to be loved. No doubt, there are people who support us and lift us up in this quest. But we also encounter people who make this very difficult. Each negative comment and hurtful act that we experience may chip away at our self-esteem. Heartache after heartache, we can become a little cracked. Until one day, we simply feel broken.

Just as the severity of bullying falls on a spectrum, so do the effects. Even the more common forms of bullying, like gossip and rumors, are no walk in the park. It's not easy to just brush off these comments and pretend that everything is copacetic.

Think back to a time where someone called you something unkind. Why is it that you remember that? Because it affected you; it made an impression. Maybe with time, the impact fades, but it never completely goes away. And the results intensify the more frequently bullying occurs and the longer it persists.

Bullying can take quite an emotional toll, causing girls to feel anxious and fearful at school, not knowing what aggression awaits them. It can cause girls to feel humiliated and ashamed to simply be themselves. Bullying can cause girls to look in the mirror and hate themselves. It can cause girls to act in a way they normally wouldn't, changing who they are to avoid conflict. Bullying can cause girls to do things that don't sit well with them, just because they are afraid of what would happen if they don't. It can cause girls to shut out the rest of the world and isolate themselves so no one else can hurt them. Bullying can cause girls to lose their trust in people. It can cause girls to wish they were never born. Bullying can cause girls to cry *every single day*.

Over time, bullying can impact other areas of your life too, such as academic performance. How can a girl concentrate when her mind is elsewhere? Test scores and GPAs drop. Some individuals may start failing their classes altogether, which can impact their future plans.

Not to mention the health effects. Stress levels increase, which can cause sleep patterns and eating habits to get all out of whack. As one feels emotionally drained, she may withdraw from activities and social plans that she used to find pleasurable. Sadness can become depression. Nervousness can lead to the onset of anxiety disorders. Girls may try to release their pain through unhealthy means, such as alcohol, drugs, self-harming, or eating disorders.

Then there is suicide. Young people have taken their own lives as a result of the endless torment they faced. These tragic stories make headlines regularly: Phoebe Prince, 15; Ryan Halligan, 13; Amanda Todd, 15; Tyler Clementi, 18; Ashlynn Conner, *10*, just to name a few.

No one should be made to feel that suicide is their only escape. Everyone should feel loved and safe.

We can't downplay the long-term consequences of bullying either. We get so caught up in the present, we fail to realize the impact that our *daily* actions and words have in the *future*. Teens don't easily outgrow the pain of bullying; it lasts into adulthood. An apology may make things better, but it doesn't erase what happened.

The effects of group bullying are also detrimental to a person's self-worth and identity. Group bullying occurs when it's one person against what feels like an *army* of aggressors. For whatever reason, peers cluster together and do something as a group that hurts one targeted person.

When I was in high school, I found out that a few girls from my grade had a Facebook chat group to discuss all the things they didn't like about me. I read it. While I've certainly made my fair share of mistakes, I knew in my heart that I didn't deserve that kind of treatment. No one does. Yet it was so hard *not* to let the things they were saying as they bashed me and picked me apart hurt.

I remember scanning the names of the people in the group and being surprised because I did not have close friendships with several of them. All I could think was, *What did I do to that girl? Why on earth would she be participating in this?* What hurt even more were the comments from people I was close with.

One girl in particular was my very best friend. I never knew she thought all of those horrible things about me and I wish she would have talked to me about it, instead of sharing her feelings with everyone else *but* me. Out of all the comments, hers hurt the most because we had been such great friends for so long. Even now, I can feel the tightness in my chest, burning in my cheeks, and the racing of my heart, as if it were happening all over again. That's how much it hurt me.

As hard as it was to experience, I learned a lot from this incident. While going through something like that, you learn things about yourself that need to change and you also realize that who you surround yourself with plays a *major* role in your happiness and in your life. You start to realize what actually is important in a friend. Trust me when I say, it *does not* matter who is cool, what group someone is in, or what their social status is. All that stuff fades. What matters the most is how they treat *you*.

So if you're "friends" with a group of girls who don't always treat you well or who make decisions with a pack mentality, rather than as individuals, break free from that group. Seek out new friendships. That is the *best* choice you can make for yourself in that situation. It may be hard or uncomfortable at first, but those are not real friends. Ultimately, it's *you* who gets to decide who you want to spend time with. Look for quality people who won't sit around bashing you and picking out your flaws, and getting enjoyment out of it at your expense. Be friends with the girl who would stick up for you and remove themselves from that situation. Be friends with girls who you trust to have your back and who would come to you and only you if they ever had an issue. Look for the qualities in people that you admire. And look for people who have a backbone.

NOW MATTERS.

When we gossip, say something unkind, or act standoff-ish, we are *definitely* not thinking about how our actions are paving the way for what lies before us. And why would we? The present is already crazy enough, with classes, homework, sports, activities, family, friends. Why even think about the future when it's so far away and we have no control over it?

The truth is, how we treat people *today* has way more importance over *tomorrow* than we realize. While we may not have complete control over it, we definitely *do* have the power to position ourselves in ways that bring more happiness and positivity to our lives.

I am here to tell you that what happens *now* does matter. Yes, people can change and reinvent themselves, but our past selves are connected to our future selves, and that is a cord that can never really be cut.

When we get older, when we leave middle school, high school, and even college, we start thinking about who we want to be in this world. And that is influenced by *everything* we have been through in our lives: all the successes, all the failures, all the positive and negative relationships, all the times we made good decisions, and all the times we could have done things differently.

In time, the way we treated people does come back around. Perhaps you will run into someone from your past that will trigger a memory and remind you of an encounter when you weren't all that nice. *Why did I do that? Why did I leave that person out? Why did I call her a mean name?* We don't think about the effect we are having in the midst of our actions. But later in life, you do.

I remember a time in school when students were allowed to buy dedication pages in the yearbook. It was customary for friends to get a page together, filling it with pictures and inside jokes. That same "best friend" of mine, the one from the Facebook story, and I decided that we wanted to take out a page. The thing is, we were very close with another girl. The three of us were always together. We could have purchased a page together. But because my best friend and I were friends longer, we thought we shared a special bond and opted to take out a page just the two of us.

Well, as you can imagine, that really hurt our friend. And to this day, I am so, so sorry for how we acted. Because the yearbook page didn't matter. It wasn't important. But how I made my friend feel? That was important.

Bottom line: we may not think our day-to-day actions and words carry much impact but that couldn't be further from the truth. Not only do they affect the people we target, but also, they affect us down the road. Eventually we do feel the repercussions of hurting someone or treating someone unkindly. That's a consequence of bullying. Whatever temporary satisfaction one may get from targeting someone else pales in comparison to the feelings of regret you eventually feel. You realize that certain fights or conflicts really just weren't worth it.

WHAT'S THE POINT?

So if all this girl drama doesn't serve anyone, why do girls engage in relational aggression anyway? There can be a number of reasons.

Some girls may perpetrate mean acts because it makes

them feel in control. Bullying gives them an avenue to exert power over others. Or maybe girls are bored and want to create excitement. Knowing the latest gossip or telling a juicy story might give them a thrill.

Perhaps they participate in rumors or planned schemes against a girl because it makes them feel closer to and more a part of another group. In many instances, girls may feel insecure and try and cover it up by pointing out other people's flaws. If they target another girl first, they may think they are less likely to be a target themselves.

Girls will also bully someone simply because they are jealous. They may feel she is prettier, smarter, or more popular. Targeting her may make her seem less desirable to others. Jealousy is truly an evil emotion that can make girls do crazy things. While everyone will experience jealousy at some point in her life, try not to act on those impulses. Instead, wait it out, let those feelings pass, because it truly is a destructive emotion.

Sometimes a girl is mean to others because she has been the victim of bullying herself. It may be how she releases the unhappy, pent-up feelings she has inside. In bullying someone else, she is probably trying to give off a tough vibe so that girls will be more hesitant to target her, lessening her chances of being a victim again.

This is by no means an excuse for her behavior, but it can be helpful to understand why someone acts the way they do. Instead of thinking her meanness stems from being pure evil, she may have a wounded soul. People who are genuinely happy and love who they are do not have to bring others down to feel good. They just don't get a kick out of it.

LIFE OUTSIDE SCHOOL

Right now, school is your kingdom. You are focused on *everything* that goes down in its hallways, from the social scene to the sports, the clubs, and, of course, all the homework. After school gets out, everyone goes home. And it's important to remember that everyone's home life is *vastly* different. Some of you may be thinking, *Duhhhh, Trish, I already knew that.* But if we knew the reality of what another girl might be going through at home, maybe we wouldn't be so quick to roll our eyes or make her feel insecure and uncomfortable. We may share the school day together, but we have *no idea* what happens during that time we are apart.

We might walk through our front door after school and have a very different experience than someone else. While our own home life may be one that is extremely loving, supportive, and caring, we can't just assume that's the same for everyone. If you equate "family" with positive emotions and thoughts, that is a wonderful thing. Many others hear "family" and think *stress* or *dysfunction.* They may associate it with feelings of anger, sadness, frustration, or hurt. It all depends on one's experiences.

There is no shortage of reasons as to why one's household could be a difficult place to come back to after a long day at school. Maybe there is a temporary hurdle that a family is struggling to overcome, creating a stressful atmosphere. Or perhaps a girl's challenging home life is more of a permanent situation. Parents could be arguing for what seems like forever. Maybe they are going through a painful divorce. Perhaps a relative is sick. A parent could have just lost his or her job, putting a financial strain and stress on the family. Or what if both parents work long hours and a girl feels lonely? Maybe someone's family member has a harsh way of treating others? We just never know what goes on behind closed doors.

The reason I'm bringing this up is because continuous jabs and digs add up. And we have no idea how many other times a day a particular girl is the subject of them. So you may call a girl annoying and think it's no big deal. But what if, on that same day, she didn't make the cheerleading team and then signed on to Instagram and saw a picture of all her friends hanging out without her. And then she went home to cry to a parent who is super stressed out and can't talk. So she tried to go to her sister, who closed the door in her face because she had a bad day herself. That one time you call a girl a loser may just be the straw that breaks the camel's back.

The point is: we do not know what someone's threshold is. We have no idea how much hurt and emotion someone is going through or how much they can handle. And if something horrible was to happen to that girl whom we just made a dig at, if she were to do something drastic as a result of the pileup of hurt she's been feeling, could you imagine how remorseful we would feel? Instead of wishing we could rewind time and take everything back, let's try be positive in everything we do, every decision we make, every action we take, and every word we speak.

Maybe we know a girl is having problems. If it's one of our closer girlfriends, she might have shared glimpses into what is going on in her life. And if that's the case, why on earth would we kick her—or let others kick her—when she's already down? She deserves all the love and support she can get. Cut her some slack. Lift her up; don't bring her down. But what if the girl is not someone we are friends with? What if you notice there is a girl at school who is on the constant receiving end of name-calling and is regularly left out? Maybe people are scared to be seen with her because everyone thinks she's a "freak" or a "weirdo." So everyone ignores her. Have you ever stopped to think what else is going on in her life and what challenges she faces?

MAKE YOUR MOVE

1. FLIP IT OR ZIP IT

If you find yourself tempted to utter some not-so-nice words, *count to ten.* Don't immediately act on impulses that are negatively directed toward someone else. In those ten seconds, ask yourself: Is this action worth it? Can I say this more nicely? Take some time to consider what you want to say/do, how you want to say/do it, and what the consequences are. If you can't flip it to something nicer, zip it. We have to treat others with the respect and kindness that we want for ourselves.

2. STAND UP

Nobody likes to be treated badly. The sly, underhanded ways girls get at one another is mean—and it hurts. We cannot let these catty, harmful behaviors go under the radar while we sit back passively. It's time to stand up and speak out. People need *our* help.

Think about it: If you were being bullied, wouldn't you want someone to help you? What if it was your sister or brother? Wouldn't you want someone to intervene? If you do your part and the next person does theirs, it will cause a positive chain reaction in how we treat each other. Bullies will be stopped and there will be fewer victims.

Fear often prevents girls from acting—fear that if they stick up for someone, they will become the next target, that they will be made fun of or that their friends will turn on them. I understand that fear. There was a time in middle school when I was afraid to go against my friends. Remember what we said about true friends? Would they turn on you for lending a helping hand?

Do the *right* thing, even if it's not the *popular* thing. Just one person, one action, can change—or maybe even save— someone's life. So stand up. You will look back and be so proud of yourself.

3. GET HELP

You can also stop bullying by bringing it to the attention of an adult.

If you are being bullied, don't keep it to yourself for fear that saying something would make matters worse or because you think no one will believe you. Courage does not come from suffering in silence. Courage is having the strength to ask for help when you need it.

If you witness someone being bullied or if you know that certain classmates are making someone's life very difficult, don't keep it a secret. There *are* people to turn to for help.

4. REACH OUT

Another way to help is to reach out to the person who is being targeted. They likely feel alone and isolated, as if they have nobody by their side. A simple *hello* and *how are you* can brighten someone's day. So can a compliment. Do you like another girl's shoes? Did she make a great play during gym class or have a great answer in science? A little kindness can alleviate the pain someone is experiencing. Invite her to sit with you at lunch or include her in plans, like going for coffee or fro yo. By reaching out, you show that you care. You show that this girl is *seen*. Extend a hand. Make a difference. After all, wouldn't you like someone to do the same for you?

5 FACEBOOK, INSTAGRAM, TWITTER, OH MY!

Welcome to the world of social networking—enter at your own risk.

Back in the olden days (sorry, Mom!), girls primarily only had to worry about bullies, conflict, and drama with friends during school hours. They didn't have other means of communication to keep the juicy gossip flowing. Enter the era of cell phones, text messages, and the Internet with Instagram, Twitter, Facebook, Snapchat, and other outlets that give us girls access to pretty much anybody at any time or anyplace we like. All of these platforms also provide additional avenues for negativity and bullying…and let me tell you, girls get creative.

I bet the majority of us can remember seeing posts on one of those social networking sites that we wish we hadn't seen. Whether it was a picture posted of all your friends (except for you) that made you feel left out and or a sarcastic, insulting comment that you knew was an indirect dig at you, we've all felt that sudden pang of hurt, sadness, or embarrassment from something we've seen online.

The truth of the matter is: the Internet is *always* open for business. That means twenty-four hours a day, seven days a week, girls can use social networking sites to judge, exclude, belittle, attack, harm, hurt, insult, and make fun of others. While there's no doubt that being on the receiving end of an attack feels terrible, we sometimes forget just how much we—sometimes unintentionally—participate in the vicious cycle.

In this chapter, we'll take a deeper look into cyberbullying (yes, any negativity through a phone or on the Internet, no matter how small it seems, *is* cyberbullying), how we are getting swept into potentially destructive patterns, how to deal with those wish-you-never-received-them text messages, how to handle the ugly side of social networking sites, and finally, how to embrace the positive side of social networking sites.

FACELESS

If we're really being honest, I think we could all admit that girls have way more courage to make negative comments over the Internet or from their cell phones than they would in person. It's easier to be aggressive and harsh when you aren't face-to-face. Our phones and computers do the dirty work while we stay hidden behind a screen. We are shielded from the girl on the other side when we don't have to look her in the eye and see the sadness and hurt we've inflicted. Cell phones don't cry; computer screens don't feel pain.

From the day we get our first cell phones, those babies are always by our sides. Before we know it, our phones become our predominant way of communicating, and our messages become a little gutsier. It's easy to get sucked into that habit given the thirty thousand times a day we use our phone.

But if you find yourself being more rude with more 'tude in text messages or online, it's time to pump the brakes. Ultimately that behavior does more harm than good. Not only can this habit make us less compassionate, but it also sets the stage for how we handle in-person interactions in the future. What happens when you have to resolve a conflict immediately and directly? Will your knee-jerk reaction be abrasive, or will you pause and respond calmly? If you have relied on your phone to be a buffer in uncomfortable conversations, your response may not reflect well on you. Another challenge in not conversing face-to-face is having to interpret the tone behind someone's message. This can be a complete guessing game! *How is she saying that? Is she really being harsh, or is she just joking? Was that said seriously or sarcastically?* It can get unnecessarily confusing to try to figure out how a message was supposed to be received. Instead of wasting all that mental energy, why not just send messages that are straightforward?

Many times girls *do* send messages that are intended to be mean, but they use ambiguous tone thing to their advantage.

Then they can say, "It was just a joke. You're taking it the wrong way." Now all of a sudden, the blame is put on the recipient of the text, not the person who sent it. When did we have to become text-message-interpreting ninjas? Since we can't hear the tone in somebody's voice, meaning gets misconstrued all the time. Your best bet is to play it safe and tone it down!

NAMELESS

The anonymity the Internet offers can be particularly appealing to teens. From making up fake accounts or using a blocked number to make old-school prank calls, we've become so skilled in avoiding detection or blame! We are like little technological masterminds. Proceed with caution. Anonymity brings out the *very worst* in people. Your identity may be hidden, but your words ring loud and clear to the victims. They still make an impact.

It's worth mentioning that even fake accounts and unsigned messages can be traced back to you in a cyber-investigation. If push comes to shove, there *are* ways to find out who is behind the anonymous content. You are still responsible for what you say. And what about one of your friends spilling the beans? Many times at least one person knows about someone's secretive alter ego.

The take-home message here is this: inflicting injury from a distance, from behind a "mask," is *not cool* and is harmful.

WHAT EXACTLY IS CYBERBULLYING?

Where do you draw your digital line? When does "normal" online behavior cross over to the dark side? Let me break down cyberbullying for you. It is any action taken by someone via a technology platform that is done *deliberately* with the *intention* of harming another person. Now, cyberbullying can look different depending on the technology used (computer, cell phone, iPad, etc.), the outlet of choice (texting, phone calls, Facebook, etc.), and the motive. The severity of cyberbullying varies, yet regardless of the degree, there are very real and harmful consequences. Harming someone includes the intention to be mean, belittle, embarrass, make fun of, humiliate, put down, exclude, hurt, and threaten.

If we find ourselves angry, hurt, or jealous, all it takes is a glance at the phone, a few typed words, and then *boom*: we've sent out messages or comments to let off some steam and, if we're being honest, perhaps even retaliate. It's so easy to forget the power that stems from each and every word we type. Hurtful comments or actions that come from our phones, not our mouths, are still considered bullying.

True, maybe you didn't scream in someone's face or physically hurt someone, but your instant messages and posts are an extension of *you*. With every Like button pressed, comment sent, and message posted, you give people a taste of who you are and what you stand for. When you're being unkind and hurtful in those spaces, that *is* bullying. Regardless of how a message was delivered, however incognito it may be, the source's intent to hurt the recipient is all that matters. Whatever form the aggression takes, be it a tweet, a comment, or a status update, the laptop or phone is not responsible for the attack—we are.

NEWSWORTHY

Cyberbullying is certainly an issue, but do you ever stop and think about *just* how problematic it is? I definitely don't want to put you to sleep with stats, but it's important to understand the prevalence of cyberbullying and how it affects teens all over the world. Let's get those beautiful minds a-thinkin' and talk facts.

According to Ditch the Label, an antibullying organization, which has conducted the largest cyberbullying survey to date (more than ten thousand teens from all across the world), seven in ten young people are victims of cyberbullying and 40 percent of youths experience cyberbullying on a frequent basis. Wow—that's a lot! This has been found to have catastrophic effects on the self-esteem and social lives of those affected. Facebook, ask.fm, and Twitter were said to be common forums for this bullying.

Additionally, the PEW Internet Research Center revealed that 95 percent of social media–using teens who have witnessed cruel behavior on social networking sites say they have seen others ignoring the mean behavior. And it's not just that people ignore this behavior; 66 percent of teens who witnessed cyberbullying also witnessed others joining in.

The consequences of such behavior are alarming. **Cyberbullying can get *very ugly*.**

If you're experiencing a cyberbullying attack, it's important to act promptly and seriously. Do *not* engage in dialogue or retaliate. This is so crucial. Like instigators, cyberbullies are on the hunt for a reaction. When you don't give it to them, you take away their power. Many times they will lose interest and move on.

Next, *tell someone*. Adapt a zero-tolerance pact against cyberbullying. You don't deserve the hurt it causes. Tell an adult: a parent, teacher or guidance counselor, family friend, religious adviser, police officer, *someone*. They can help you. Many social networking sites also have the option to report an incident. Don't think that there is nothing you can do about cyberbullying. If it is happening to you, make sure to act.

Save, record, and/or print any instances of cyberbullying. Don't let attacks persist. People can go back and delete what they said or posted. If the comment or action was threatening and harmful, it's safe to have documentation of it.

THE INTERNET'S BETTER HALF

The Internet and social networking sites do not have to be places of negativity or sources of drama. A lot of good can come from them as well. Social networking sites are great ways to spread positive information. Articles about heroic acts and miraculous news stories can reach an enormous audience. Uplifting quotes and news about charities and people who do good in the world inspire others to take positive and loving action in their own lives. The Internet is also home to beautiful, supportive communities. So which group do you want to be a part of?

One of my favorite stories is about a gem of a girl who took a stance on cyberbullying by using her Facebook account in a positive way. Each day, this middle school student chose a different person in her grade and wrote a kind comment on his or her wall. She continued writing compliments until she had said something nice about every person in her grade.

Her classmates caught on and decided to do the same, creating a domino effect. At the end of a day, the students from this particular school could get online and receive more than thirty notifications, each post including something positive about them from someone they see almost every day.

How cool is that? How good would it feel to receive all those positive messages? And how good would it feel to write those compliments about your classmates?

This story really touched me. I saw the level of good that could come from these sites and reflected on how I was using social media. I thought about what kind of content I had on my accounts, how my overall energy and attitude came across, and who I chose to follow. I decided I could step up my love game, and since then, I've made a conscious effort to use all of my accounts in a more positive way. I want my online presence to reflect the type of person I am, whom I choose to surround myself with, and what I stand for. And for me, that means no negativity and no hate.

It's time to take a look at your accounts to see what kind of content you are putting out into the world. Looking truthfully at our behaviors and actions takes a lot of courage, but let's get honest *now*, so we can blaze into the future as a shinier, hipper version of ourselves.

MAKE YOUR MOVE

1. RAISE YOUR VIBE

Whether we realize it or not, everyone exudes a certain type of energy. I'm not talking about one's physical energy level, but more about that *feeling* you get when you're around certain people. In other words, the vibe they give off. People can either lift you up by being happy, fun individuals who you enjoy being around (a.k.a. high vibers) or people can make you feel out of sorts by either being negative or by doing things that don't sit well with you (a.k.a. the low vibers).

As I mentioned before, your online presence is an extension of you. So not only do we give off a vibe, but our activity on the Internet does as well. I want you to ask yourself what kind of vibes you are giving off on these sites. Is it high vibe or low vibe?

Example: complimenting someone's picture = *high vibe*.

Not tagging someone in a group photo = *low vibe*.

I want you to think deeply about how you are using

your social networking sites. Do you judge or criticize? Have you been flaunting or bragging? How much stalking did you do this week? (Yes, LOL, we've all achieved stalker status at some point or another.)

Take a step back. What does a viewer see when they look at your sites? How would they describe you from your accounts? It's easy to call out people who are being hurtful and insulting, especially if we are the target. We know who tends to post unkind stuff, whether it is blatantly obvious or a little more discreet, and we know who judges and puts others down. But it's important to remember that if we Like someone's status or picture when we know it is really a dig at someone else, or if we share a negative post, then we are contributing to the problem. We are perpetuating the cycle.

Once you identify which one you are, even if you're a high viber, dare to raise it up. Don't settle on "meh." I want those vibe meters at an all-time high. Every action you take via your cell phone and online, stop and ask yourself: Is this high vibe? This is a great opportunity to make a massive shift in the way you communicate and portray yourself *for the better*. Actively make your sites more positive, reach out to others in a kinder way, share nicer content. I applaud you for any positive changes you make here!

2. CLEAR OUT
Next, let's minimize the drama and gossip that you are exposed to online. I strongly encourage you to unfollow

or unfriend anyone who bursts your happy bubble. Now, you might be hesitant to unfriend someone you see on a regular basis because it could cause a problem in your social circle. I get that. If it will cause drama, then don't. At the very least, try not to wander onto their pages or block them from showing up on your news feed (you can do this on Facebook), so you won't automatically see the low-vibe stuff unless you go fishing for it.

If you aren't in that position and someone is constantly putting out unkind, low-vibe stuff, then delete them. Their content is *not serving you*. Negativity has a way of seeping into our subconscious, leaving us with a funky feeling that we can't quite place. Don't we have enough stuff on our plate anyway? We definitely don't need to be brought down by reading someone's negative Facebook status.

3. UP THE GOODS!

Now that we've gotten rid of the negative, let's *up the positive*! Increase the number of people you follow who put positive content on the Internet. Follow more of your favorite bands, celebrities, athletes, or people who genuinely inspire you. Personally, I'm a huge fan of inspirational quotes. They help me to refocus and keep perspective on what actually matters in life, so I don't get caught up in the catty stuff.

Not everyone you follow and interact with has to be in your age-group or from a nearby community either. There are plenty of sources of inspiration from people older than you, from all over the world, who have gone through many similar and different experiences, and who can provide truly meaningful advice. Seek out some Internet role models.

As we've learned in this chapter, the Internet has its pitfalls, but it also has its perks. We can't change how other people use their social networking sites, but we can change how we use ours, making them positive extensions of ourselves. We all have to do our part and *commit to deleting the digital drama*. Let's tweet that.

6 FREE YOURSELF

There's always a current of drama at school. Sometimes the water is calm, while other times it gets real choppy. When we hit the storm and the drama comes in full blast, it can feel like too much to handle. We start questioning why girls have to be so mean. Is school supposed to be this difficult? Why didn't we get a warning? Maybe part of you hopes for an easier, more enjoyable ride; hopes that there's got to be another way, so everyone can act nicer, friendlier. And as always, your intuition is right.

Fresh starts are like massages for the soul. What better way is there to get over the drama that's bringing you down than to face it, learn from it, release it, and start over? Fresh starts get down to the deep issue, work some magical transformation, and then leave us feeling all Zen and happy.

Unfortunately, many of us cling to long-standing, deep-rooted grudges from our past. But the longer these resentments continue to replay in our present lives, the more we subconsciously repeat the same negative patterns. It's time to clear that space for a positive shift. It's time to let go of the stuff that's weighing us down. This chapter will help you clean out your emotional baggage, so you can make room for all of the good that you want in your life, like love, happiness, laughs, and really good people—just to name a few!

DROP RESENTMENTS

The moment we decide that we don't like another girl, we section off a part of our minds and assign them the job of fostering that dislike. They become hate zones that are home to all our negative thoughts. It's as if there's an electrical fence that shocks away any positive feelings we might have toward that person. We cringe when we hear her name. If a friend says, "Oh, she really isn't that bad," we instantly shut it down and could probably fill a good hour explaining our reasoning. Bottom line: we don't like her. End of story.

We underestimate the power of the resentment. Rather than cutting ties with someone, resentments build a strong connection between you and whomever you dislike. All of your thoughts and feelings about her become infused with bitterness. The longer these resentments last, the more they become ingrained and the harder it is to move on.

Sure, you may not like whatever has happened between the two of you, the feelings that came out of it, and the girl who is behind it. But think long and hard before you put a girl into that hate zone. Let the anger pass, let the storm settle, and then act. There is a difference between not wanting to be close to someone and having a full-out blind rage for them. And if you chose the path of resentment, you are only punishing yourself. Because that's what resentment does.

Resentment blocks you. It keeps you from receiving happiness, from laughing really hard, from loving yourself completely. Love can't exist where hate is running the show. Resentment is like a backpack that is stuffed with textbooks; it's heavy and it drags you down. The second you take that backpack off, you will be lighter, more carefree. Let go of grudges. Redirect that energy toward a hobby, other friendships, anything that makes you smile and energizes you. Life will be so much more enjoyable!

BE OPEN TO A DIFFERENT DYNAMIC

You may be thinking, *All right, Trish. This sounds great and all, but I don't think you understand how much I do not like this girl. I can't just let it go and put on a happy face.*

I totally get where you're coming from. We're human. We have intense emotions. And doing a total 180 doesn't just happen overnight. Believe me, I wish I had some special fairy dust that we could sprinkle to make all our resentments go away. That would be *a lot* easier.

I'm suggesting a *willingness* to reevaluate the situation. Own how you feel, but say, *I'm really angry about this, but*

I'm willing not to be. That little bit of flexibility can go a long way toward seeing things differently. Open up your heart, even if a tiny bit, to welcome in her good. It doesn't mean that you ignore her part in the situation, but it does mean that you chose to see beyond a person's flaws.

Welcome change. It's totally okay if you don't know what that change might look like or feel like. After all, there can be layers and layers of built-up anger to bust through. If you've felt wronged, chances are frustrations about the situation have added to that wall. My advice is to be open to possibility. Because that negative energy that you've been harboring, believe it or not, is perpetuating more of her attacks. It's a cycle. A little bit of generosity to see things in a different light can break that behavior.

That is because people respond to other people's energy. When someone is happy, they are easy to be around. But when they are tense and standoffish, well, that's another story. And of course, when we don't like someone, nine times out of ten, it's easy to tell because of the energy we are giving off.

Shifting the dynamic doesn't require a grandiose gesture where angel wings shoot out of your back and you suddenly love her to pieces. But if you are open and nice and share a smile or a compliment, your overall demeanor and mood will change for the positive. It will defuse the situation and encourage a positive response. I wouldn't be a bit surprised if that girl were nicer to you. That can help you release the anger you have felt toward her.

At the end of the day, *we* have the final say in how we feel about others. The anger and bitterness within us is not the other person's fault, no matter what they did. Anytime we hold a grudge against someone, we must take responsibility for our emotions and actions.

Do we really want to use all of our energy on those we consider enemies? It is so much nicer to be able to walk down the hallway and smile at everyone. Be open to positive encounters. Look for the good in everyone and you'll be able to walk into any room and see friends—and potential new friends.

HAPPINESS > BEING RIGHT

When we feel really wronged by someone, our first instinct is to go on the defense. An imaginary wall goes up in our minds and our hearts, protecting us from that person while we figure out our next step. Some of us may take on the victim role, where we feel personally preyed upon by another girl, making her guilty for everything that went down. Others may immediately respond through retaliation. If someone hurts them, they waste no time fighting back. Others might shut down and completely shy away from the person and the incident. The last thing they want to do is get hurt by more conflict. It's hard to break these patterns. When we're wronged, we get mad, we feel hurt, and we want an apology!

What happens if that apology doesn't come? In many

instances, it doesn't (at least not in the way that we expect or as genuinely as we think we deserve). And if that's the case, it's pretty hard to shake the not-so-nice feelings we have toward that girl. We dig in our heels. We won't change our minds or welcome another opinion. "No, I'm right. She's wrong. I'm not talking to her until she apologizes." Sound familiar? We get so stuck on having to prove that we are right that we close ourselves to other viewpoints or explanations.

We can bend over backward to get others to see how wronged we were, yet in the end, that still doesn't get us anywhere. Even if we do get that desired stamp of approval that indeed we were "right," what happens next? We didn't resolve the conflict or get an apology. We just got confirmation from others that we were right and a pat on the back to go with it.

What if we choose to be happy? That would mean that we're not fighting to prove that we are right or that we're better than another girl. Instead we're free to focus on what makes us happy. We can choose to enjoy our lives and all the amazing things in it, instead of maintaining conflicts. When you choose happiness over being right, your priorities change and you can focus your energy on what's important to you.

F IT!

Yes, you read correctly. I said, F it! And by F it, of course I mean **Forgive it!**

If you're in a major fight with someone and are off the

charts angry, you might react by saying something like, *"No, I will absolutely, 100 percent, no way forgive her!"* Before you make up your mind, put your foot down, or skip ahead, I'm asking you to step back and take a few minutes; stay with me here.

There's a reason why so many books about conflict resolution between friends recommend forgiveness. Parents, teachers, and counselors all suggest it. Religious leaders, yogis, and spiritual teachers seek peace *as their job*, and they recommend forgiveness. Why? It's because they have all experienced its healing benefits firsthand. And if all of these people have something good to say about forgiveness, then maybe we shouldn't be so quick to rule it out.

So what is holding us back from saying the F word? Most likely, we want to protect ourselves. By withholding our forgiveness, we may think we are keeping ourselves safe so we are no longer vulnerable. And we may not *want* to be compassionate toward someone who has hurt us. We don't want to do something nice for them. Which brings me to our first point…

MYTH #1: FORGIVENESS IS ONLY DONE FOR THE OTHER PERSON.

That is false! Yes, when you let go of your anger toward another, it releases them. But the act of forgiving also frees you. Living with resentment causes you pain and unhappiness. And the longer you cling to those feelings, the more you relive the past with a closed mind and a vengeful heart, keeping your wounds open.

Forgiveness allows you to live in the moment, without the weight of past mistakes. You owe it to yourself to let go of anger so you can live your life happily and peacefully. If you can't convince yourself to forgive for the other person, convince yourself to do it for you.

MYTH #2: FORGIVENESS MEANS THAT WHAT THE OTHER PERSON DID WAS ACCEPTABLE.

Nope! Just because you forgive someone's actions doesn't mean you approve of what they did. Forgiveness does not mean being BFF or going back to the way things were either. You don't have to hang out or even necessarily talk. Instead, it means you wipe the slate clean and let go of the past. Respect one another and be kind whenever your paths cross. It's as simple as that.

MYTH #3: FORGIVING PEOPLE MAKES YOU A DOORMAT.

That couldn't be further from the truth. Those who are forthright and firm in their anger can come across as tough, which tends to be respected. But that doesn't make them strong; it just makes them immovable. Sometimes it shows more strength to let go than it does to hold on. The person who extends forgiveness is strong and brave. She can accept responsibility for her role in what happened and release the blame from herself and from others.

Forgiveness takes time and it takes practice. You have to strengthen that ability like a muscle. The stronger the skill gets, the easier it will be to lift up problems and release them. And the more you extend forgiveness, the more natural it becomes. You regroup from difficult situations faster. Forgiveness is truly at the heart of feeling better and moving forward. And remember, there is no situation that forgiveness cannot heal.

SEE IT AND SAY IT WITH LOVE

We don't always get to decide what happens in our lives, but we do have a choice in how we perceive those events. We can see them with love or we can see them with hate.

Essentially, you can view situations with empathy and compassion or you can understand them in a way that further brings you down.

For example, say a girl calls you a mean name, which makes you feel terrible. Your first instinct may be something like: *I am so pissed off! I hate her!* You might then call her something mean in return.

What if we didn't do that? What if our first instinct was to think: *Wow, she must be going through something difficult to lash out like that. I'm going to muster up some compassion and let this one slide. I am choosing to forgive her and not let her comment impact me.* How would that change the dynamic?

We cannot change what was said or done. How we respond, however, has a *major* influence on how we feel about what happened. When we choose to react with anger, we get stressed, tense, possibly even a little scary, and we might take a brief vacation to Crazytown. But when we choose to show love, we get calmer and happier, and we regain control over how we feel instead of letting another person's actions dictate that for us.

And those people who *really* get under your skin, *really* test your patience, and are *really* hard for you to like? They are your greatest teachers. They will challenge you to extend your capacity for compassion. They will push you to be more loving and more forgiving. Accept the challenge!

So the next time someone says something unkind, how will you respond? I hope that you'll show as much love as you can, because every girl has a story. And although they may not have penned theirs in kindness, you get to decide how yours will be written.

MAKE YOUR MOVE

TO FORGIVE OR NOT TO FORGIVE? THAT IS THE QUESTION

In order to make the right decision, a little homework is needed. (Don't worry. You'll know all the answers.)

Start by picking one girl who evokes the strongest negative reaction in you. Below is a list of questions to answer about what went down between you two.

Grab a journal and write down your responses. This is for your eyes only, so vent and let it all out. This is a safe place to work through your thoughts and emotions, rather than gossiping about them with others.

I encourage you to do this assignment for anyone who you have a long-standing dislike and bad feelings toward. Note: I know this may look like a lot of work, but it really doesn't take long—and it is important! You'll be so much happier when you do.

1. Who is the girl: _____

2. What happened between the two of you?

3. When did this happen?

4. How did it make you feel? (Angry, sad, embarrassed, etc.)

5. Do you still have those feelings? To what extent?

6. Why are you hesitant to forgive her and mend
   things between you?

7. How has the situation affected you? (Self-
   esteem, confidence, trust, etc.)

8. Put yourself in the other girl's shoes. Why do
   you think she acted the way she did?

9. What is your part in this? Be honest. How
   might you have contributed to (or escalated)
   the situation?

10. What is one pleasant memory you have with
    this person?

11. What is one positive characteristic about her?
    (Yes, I assure you, there is at least one!)

12. Now that we've discussed forgiveness and
    how it benefits everyone involved, can you
    forgive this girl? What steps can you take to
    do that?

THINGS TO KEEP IN MIND:

- ♡ Every person, every situation can teach us something new and help us grow.
- ♡ Everyone goes through a rough patch.
- ♡ Every day is an opportunity to start fresh.
- ♡ Sometimes to forgive others, you need to forgive yourself first.

Psst... Did you figure out the answer? Forgive!

DAMAGE CONTROL

In all the years we spend in school, you'd think we would become experts on how to handle drama. Situations are always escalating more than they need to. An insignificant incident or the smallest remark suddenly turns into the biggest deal ever. How can we stop that? With some Conflict Resolution 101!

Girls tend to gravitate toward the soap opera script when dealing with conflict. I'm talking overly dramatic lines, yelling, exaggerated hand gestures, and some really tense facial expressions. What ever happened to having a calm conversation? To be honest, I don't think the majority of us know how to handle controversy in a way that keeps the situation contained and mellow. They're not really skills that are taught in school, and while we may learn them from our parents and other adults in our lives, it can be hard to put those skills into practice when a girl at school is being a real pain.

Whenever there is tension in the air, you can bet the chances are high that it will turn into some type of heated interaction. Almost all instances are blown out of proportion and so much so that the aftermath creates enemies, long-lasting resentments, and distrust. The thing is, the girl or girls involved *still* go to your school, you *still* see them on a regular basis, and they are *still* going to be part of your immediate surroundings until we graduate. It's super hard to escape the animosity that follows a dramatic argument and a friendship breakup. So how we respond to conflict has *way* more importance in our daily lives than we might initially acknowledge. It's all about the approach you take, and that's what we are going to talk about in this chapter. Many of us might be tempted to retaliate or just avoid the problem altogether, but that is bound to backfire. Attacking an aggressor or dodging an argument doesn't really address the problem. Unresolved conflict will snowball into more hurt feelings over time. We need to respond in a way that keeps the drama to a minimum, that sets us up for the best-case-scenario resolution, and that ultimately leaves everyone feeling as good as possible.

While the outcome is also dependent on how the other person responds to conflict, there are still steps we can take to ensure that things get resolved quickly. This chapter has valuable steps to help you handle conflict or issues with your friends. You are bound to be hurt or upset by another girl's actions at some point, so we all should know what to say or how to approach the situation when that time comes.

So take a deep breath (yes, actually breathe) and let's tackle this together!

JUST ROLE WITH IT

The first thing you need do is pinpoint exactly who you are upset with and why. Sometimes it's very obvious, but other times, it's not so clear. For example, say a group of girls are behind the action that upset us. We get mad at all of them, when really it was just one or two girls who were responsible. The others may have only been involved by association. It's hard to think of each girl as separate when they are so closely connected, but we can't fault them for what their other friends did.

Next, it's time to try and figure out the role you had in the situation. Everyone plays a part. It's human nature to go on the defensive when you've been hurt. We think that we are being unjustly attacked. Sometimes that is true, but in most cases we aren't 100 percent the victim. This step is all about owning our actions and words. It's not every day that people have the courage to say, "Hey, you know what? I really messed up and I'm sorry." Or "Yes, it really hurt me when you did ___, but it probably hurt you when I did ___. And for that, I apologize."

So before you get upset, I want you to ask yourself: What was my part in this? Did I do anything that might have perpetuated her actions? This requires *a lot* of honesty. Do a little soul searching, some self-reflection. You may realize, *Oh wow, maybe she did that to me because of x, y, z.* Understanding the situation from the other person's viewpoint can help put the situation into perspective.

For example, say one of our friends invites a bunch of people over but we weren't invited. That always stings. Maybe she didn't invite us because we didn't invite her to a get-together we had at our house a few months before. We can't hold people to a different standard than we hold ourselves. Although it's really hard to admit our part in a situation, especially when we feel offended or hurt by what someone else did, it is extremely admirable to own the role we played instead of pointing the finger or blaming someone for an issue that may not be entirely her fault.

Maybe your part is holding on to anger and hurt that is building resentment between you and a friend. Perhaps you are still unwilling to move past it, let it go, or have a conversation to say what's on your mind. Take responsibility and acknowledge that. It will help you move forward.

I applaud you for getting honest with yourself—this is a hard step!

SPEAK UP

There have definitely been times when I shied away from saying what was on my mind, only to find that those bad feelings surfaced whenever I saw the person whom I felt hurt by. I tried to avoid the hurt and the awkwardness of confronting a friend, but that didn't make me feel any better. In hindsight, I wish I had said what was on my mind *when it happened* so I could move on from the situation. Getting relief and resolution from something that hurt you is **extremely** important. No matter how uncomfortable or on-edge you might feel about talking to the other person, trust that any type of closure is better than none. Keep in mind that if you let a situation go that really upset you without discussing it, that person might get the impression that they can do or say whatever they want without regard for your feelings. It is so important that you set a clear boundary and protect yourself from anyone who seems to be constantly throwing digs at you.

Anytime that you are upset or offended by what someone did, you have every right to tell them how you feel and to let them know how hurtful their action was. However, it has to be in a *calm* and *nice* manner. Always. Under *no* circumstance should we lash out, get all our friends to turn on that person, spread nasty gossip, or "make them pay." That is never okay, no matter what they did. Those reactions just make a problem bigger *every single time*. No one will get relief from the situation or resolve the issue.

Really, when someone hurts you, you want them to acknowledge what they did, how it made you feel, and say they're sorry. And a calm, cool, and collected approach is more likely to yield that result. And just as important as *how* we have the conversation is *why* we have the conversation. Which leads me to…

MAKE PEACE NOT WAR

Let's figure out exactly how to go about having this kind of conversation. Before you decide to talk to the girl(s) involved, ask yourself: What am I looking to get out of this conversation? It can be as simple as having your feelings acknowledged and gaining closure. Maybe it's to fix a problem in your relationship, so you can go back to being besties. Hold that intention close to your heart so that when the time comes to try and resolve the issue, how you act and what you say will be in complete alignment with that goal. And whatever your aim, look to make peace not war.

1:1

The next step is planning how and when to talk to them. The most important tip to keep in mind is to *always* keep the conversations one to one. There is power in numbers and people will feel intimidated if they sit down alone while the other person has friends with them. I know it's reassuring to have someone with you for support, but it's uncomfortable for the other person who is solo. So make sure that you guys agree to talk one-on-one and if there is more than one person involved in the situation, have your own separate conversations with each of them. Definitely don't talk to both girls at the same time because they will likely defend each other more strongly, and be less open and responsive to what you have to say. And of course, only talk to the people involved in the situation or else it will get blown *way* out of proportion.

When you finally talk about what happened, make sure that the conversation takes place in person! It's *so* tempting to text instead of speak face-to-face, but there are about a million reasons why that is *not* a good idea. Texting definitely has its perks, I won't deny that. It's a lot less intimidating, as our cell phones can't exactly yell at us and we're less likely to censor ourselves, but we need to have a better relationship with *people,* not our cell phones.

Talking in person is the most mature and effective way to handle any sort of bad feelings or issues. Not to mention, anyone who suggests doing that appears calm and collected. Face-to-face conversations also have the highest potential to defuse a situation. They completely bypass the frustration of opening such a rude, blunt text. That's not to say that people aren't mean in person, but they tend to be a lot less mean than if they were communicating online or from their phone. Face-to-face conversations get to the point a lot quicker, without the unnecessary layer of drama and attitude that is so often infused in text messages.

"I DO"

One simple step when speaking with someone can *totally* change an entire conversation and prevent it from taking a turn for the worse. What is this secret? When you want to express how you feel to a friend, use "I" statements. "*I* felt really hurt when _____ happened." It will create a *big* change in how the other person feels and responds.

Constantly starting sentences with "you," "you," "you" is accusatory and puts the other person on the defensive right from the start. Would you want to sit down with someone who is listing off all of these things that you've done wrong? I would definitely feel bombarded and defensive!

Even if the other person is at fault, there are certainly ways for us to express how we feel without pointing out all of their flaws and mistakes. When we say, "This made me feel…" instead of "*You* made me feel…" it puts the attention on the effects of the actions, which is a completely different kind of conversation.

In doing so, you will elicit a response in the person that is much more desirable. They will be more open and receptive to your feelings and more likely to listen to what you have to say, as opposed to being closed off, guarded, and unwilling to understand your perspective. The majority of times, the real conflict is about feelings anyway, not necessarily facts. You can argue about facts all day long and exchange opinions on what you both think happened. When it comes down to it, people just want to be heard and they want their feelings to be acknowledged. Keeping the conversation centered on your feelings as well as caring about the other person's is key to talking about and resolving conflict. That is way more important and productive than trying to get someone to accept blame.

R&R

This next step in addressing any kind of issue or controversy takes a great deal of restraint but works in our favor *every* time. This R&R does not stand for rest and relaxation, although that probably sounds great right about now! In this case, it actually stands for *respond* with *restraint*. We shouldn't react. Although it may not seem like it, there is a very big difference between the two. When a situation occurs that ignites immediate and strong emotions in us, we are tempted to react right away. But when we reACT, we are literally acting on our emotions, which in a tense situation are at an all-time high. Of course we are going to say and do things that we don't mean when we are far from centered.

Whereas reacting is based on a gut reaction that is usually inappropriate and irrational, the other way contains a very vital element—stepping back. Responding with restraint gives us that time to take in a situation, collect our thoughts, control our emotions, *and then* decide the best course of action to take. When we react, our emotions run the show and we have less of a choice. When we respond, our reasoning takes more of a central role. Responding is more thoughtful and contains more logic. We *think* about how we want to respond before we do it. Conversely, reacting lets our emotions drive us forward. As much as we may want to address an emotionally charged situation ASAP, when we respond to a situation, we are able to take a better approach that prevents us from saying and doing things we later regret.

I once stumbled upon this quote by a man named Laurence Peter that is so fitting for this conversation. He said, "Speak when you are angry and you'll make the best speech you'll ever regret." If you adapt this one rule of *waiting* before reacting, your conversation will dramatically change for the better. We can communicate more effectively and directly when we tone back our emotional side. We can listen better and we can be more civil. It's all about that pause, the time in between an action and a response, when you can cool down and make a thoughtful decision about how you want to reply. We don't have to act immediately just because we have a piercing internal reaction that's dying to get out. We can control this urge by having the willpower to let it simmer down. I know it takes a great deal of self-control, but by waiting, we are really looking out for ourselves and making sure that we put our best foot forward. Even if you have to remove yourself from the situation, do whatever it takes to not react on the basis of your supercharged emotions.

Even if it's not our literal words that are tense and high-tempered, there's also our general body language, tone of voice, and other nonverbal ways of communicating that speak volumes. In fact, nonverbal communication plays a big role in addressing conflict, probably more so than the actual words. We can communicate with our facial expressions, posture, gestures, pace, tone, and intensity of voice.

These nonverbal signs tell a person what we're actually saying because they mirror how we truly feel.

When we are about to speak with someone regarding a conflict, the important thing to keep in mind is that it's not *just* what we say, but the attitude that lies behind it that is key. So even if someone says they're sorry but does so with a smirk or a sarcastic tone, we know it's not genuine and sincere. Therefore, that apology is irrelevant. What matters, instead, is the choice we decided to make going into the conversation: either to have a confrontational dialogue that is harsh and uncomfortable for both parties or a peaceful talk with an end goal of making amends and moving on. The person to whom we are speaking feels what we have chosen regardless of our words.

LEARN FROM THE PAST

It's also helpful to take a step back and think about how we've handled similar instances. In doing so, we can learn what works and what needs a little fine tuning. Is there a pattern to how we respond to drama and disagreements? What is our tendency? Are we avoiders, deniers, or aggressors? Do we not say anything at all and let the problem eat away at us? Maybe we say a little too much and then feel badly about it later. Have you ever tried to fix a problem with a friend only to have the conversation lead to more anger? The only thing worse than having a fight is having another fight after the fight! If this has happened to you before, try and pinpoint what exactly went wrong. That way we can avoid re-creating a bad situation and instead bring out more of the good!

In taking a look at our history, we might notice that our coping mechanisms involve denying or avoiding conflict and I'm sure you realize that those habits never make the issue go away. Denying your feelings is *never* good. And even though I'm all for forgiveness, I wouldn't encourage or expect you to simply let something go that has seriously hurt you without having some type of dialogue. You *deserve* to feel better. You don't deserve to have bad feelings bottled up inside you while you try to deny or avoid them. That will only cause more resentment and sadness in the long run because those feelings were minimized and never given the proper attention or acknowledgment that they needed.

There's also this misconception that letting go means being the bigger person, but that isn't always true. Not making a mountain out of a molehill is definitely admirable, but what if the situation is a mountain? Avoiding it doesn't make anyone "bigger," especially if it really hurts you! I'd be the first to admit that having to talk to another person about a disagreement is definitely nerve-racking and uncomfortable, so I understand why avoiding it does sound tempting. It's hard to be at odds with anyone and even though you could go into a conversation with good intentions, you just never know what the other person is thinking or how they will respond. That "not-knowing" part is challenging, but avoidance won't make it any better. In fact, it makes it worse.

MAKE YOUR MOVE

Conflict is unavoidable. There are bound to be moments when we are hurt or offended by what someone has done. But conflict doesn't necessarily mean a friendship is doomed. In fact, it can actually strengthen your bond and bring you two closer in the end. Learning how to deal with arguments and disagreements, rather than avoiding them, is critical! As is how we respond to them. If we're quick to anger, then we may overreact and speak unfairly, but it's important that we develop the right skills to handle conflict so that we can heal, feel better, and gain closure.

There is nothing good about unresolved feelings. They need to be addressed, but in the right way. Too often we reflect on a conversation and are upset because we didn't say exactly what we wanted to, or we said too much and now feel badly about it. At the end of the day, speaking with anger is never going to feel right in our hearts. We will start wondering how we could have done things different-ly. Instead of thinking about that *after* the conversation, we should think about it before and *during* the conversation, so we can look back and be pleased with how we handled ourselves and how we treated the other person.

It's all about the pause! When someone does something that makes our hearts drop and stomachs churn, it is so hard not to approach them right away. *Stop* and *chill*. We need a level head, so we don't unleash our inner turmoil on them (which will likely happen if our emotions are going crazy). What do we want to say? How do we want the conversation to unfold? What feeling do we want to get across? How do we want our relationship to be moving forward?

So let's figure out *your* pause. How do you fill that time in between the situation and your response? Here are some ideas. Pick one that speaks to you and then make sure to write it down in a notebook or on an index card or Post-it so you can refer back to it when you need. Come up with a few of your own!

Remember, when you are tempted to yell at someone, ask yourself: Is this going to help the situation or escalate it? Frequently, speaking softly will make an impact because people will *really* listen.

POTENTIAL PAUSERS

- ♥ **Take ten breaths.** Try it! There's a reason why so many people recommend it. I promise, it works! If you actually take *ten full, deep breaths*, there is no way you can NOT feel calmer.
- ♥ **Step away.** If you're in person and feel like you're about to reACT, politely walk away. You can revisit the conversation later when you are calm. If the drama is rising over the phone, put that baby down. Listen to music, take a shower, watch TV. Take a breather for five minutes. If not,

you'll wind up typing out a very heated message
that you wish you didn't send.

♥ **Get outside.** Go for a walk, take your pet out, relax
outside. The change in scenery can be distracting.

♥ **Listen to your favorite song.** Shut the door to
your room or put in your earbuds and turn up
the volume! Listening to your favorite tunes will
always help put you in a better frame of mind.

8 IT'S COOL TO BE DIFFERENT

One of the things that we all have in common, no matter our group of friends or how "different" we might be, is that we are all trying to find our way. We are trying to figure out who we are and how we can express ourselves. If that's not tough enough, we have our peers judging and criticizing us, pressuring us to look a certain way, act a certain way, be a certain type of person.

Everyone always says, "Be yourself." Well, what if we are still figuring out who that is? It's hard to develop a strong sense of self and maintain our confidence when people are picking us apart.

In order to be *truly* happy, we have to stay true to who we are. Your most *honest* and *real* self is *so* amazing, *so* talented, *so* worthy, and *so* beautiful. This is not just sweet talk. It's the truth. Too often, we let people and ideas of who we should be alter us into less cool versions of ourselves. Deep down, if you want to be happy, you have to be yourself, and you have to be yourself **unapologetically**.

This chapter is your chance to celebrate the real you. It's time to stop thinking that we need to change ourselves to be more like someone else. In this chapter, we'll take time to recognize our special qualities that make us who we are, and how important it is to appreciate our *true* friends.

ONE★OF★A★KIND

There is no one quite like you. With all those interesting things that you do, your quirks and mannerisms and all your habits (the good and bad ones), your interests, your hobbies, your talents, there will never be another you. Why hide or try to cover up any of the qualities that make you who you are? You should *celebrate* them every single day.

You shouldn't be afraid to express yourself. Whenever you're feeling insecure, I want you to tell yourself, "I am special and unique." *No one* can ever take that away from you.

Sometimes it can be difficult to express our individuality in school because it seems like everyone has an opinion about what we do and think. And whether we admit it or not, we have all, at some point, been influenced by these opinions. Everyone is trying so hard to fit in and be accepted. You may've even noticed a cookie-cutter formula. Maybe you've thought, *If I look like this or dress like that or join that club, then I will be noticed. I will be cooler.*

Each time we try to be someone we're not, we're quite

literally taking away our shine. On the surface we may seem to fit in more, but there's a cost. We're missing out on an opportunity to be one of a kind and are instead choosing to be one of many. And when we are not being 100 percent ourselves, any acceptance, approval, or admiration from others is fake. We are putting on a persona so others are responding to that persona.

It's sad that people would rather be the same and be accepted than be their self and be different. Sure, sharing commonalities, like interests and hobbies, is great, but mirroring someone else's interests and opinions just to be liked? That's not interesting *at all*.

You are the opposite of boring. You are spunky, fun, creative, interesting, and smart. You have talents and gifts that other people don't. You have your own unique personality and style, which is awesome. You are an original, so why try and be a *copy*?

There has to be this underlying belief that makes us think that our real selves are not good enough. That's why we feel like we have to change. We do certain things or act a certain way or gravitate toward a certain group so that we are accepted. We are scared to be alone, and that is understandable, but we shouldn't have to *try* to be anything that we are not. Being ourselves should come naturally. We shouldn't have to tweak our wardrobe or exaggerate our interests in something just because we would fit in more.

This is where I need to grab the microphone, get the surround-sound speakers, and say: My sweet friend, you are *perfect* just the way you are. Don't ever let someone make you think otherwise.

You should want your true personality to show because **there is** *nothing* **more attractive than your real, authentic self**. That is when you shine the most. That is when you are the most *beautiful*, the most *engaging*, and the most *magnetic*. If you are loud and silly, be loud and silly. If you are shy and reserved, be shy and reserved. Own it! That doesn't make you any less exciting or loveable. It's when we try and be a different version of ourselves that we become unhappy. You don't have to be anyone other than you. In fact, the world could use all the *you* you have to offer.

Throughout my life, whenever I've been the most *me*, my life has been the most successful, *in all areas...* I am so happy with who I am, I feel great in my relationships and friendships, and I feel inspired to set high goals. In that state, things have a funny way of falling into place. Writing this book, for example, has been a total blessing and was the result of being myself, even when it meant stepping away from the crowd.

Pouring your heart into something is not easy; you're being vulnerable and putting yourself up for judgment. However, when you are being yourself, when you are being the real deal, good things flow to you naturally because you're right where you need to be. When you're trying to control, manipulate, grasp, or pretend, you don't feel so great about yourself because you know you're *not being yourself*. Stuff comes up, funky feelings head your way, and you tend to be more irritable, stressed, and sad. You wonder why you can't just be happy. And that's because you've lost sight of the insanely incredible person that you are. The good news is, you can get her back.

When you stay true to yourself, you will always be happiest. It takes courage to stand your ground and be yourself. In those moments where you feel uncertain, nervous, or pressured to conform, trust your gut. Go with your instinct, even if it sets you apart. That is *always* the right decision.

You deserve all the happiness in the world. It doesn't matter what mistakes you've made in the past. You need to know that you are good enough, special enough, lovely enough, smart enough, wonderful enough just the way you are. You are pretty spectacular. And reread this paragraph any time you need a little reminder. ☺

EMBRACE DIVERSITY

Equally important in how we view our personal unique traits is how we view them in other people. We are *so* quick to label someone as "weird" or a "freak" just because they have interests or hobbies that are very different from our own. Maybe they do something that is foreign to us that we have absolutely zero interest in. Let me ask you a question: What if every single person in the world was exactly like us? Really think about that for a sec. What if every single person was just like you? Wouldn't you be so bored? I certainly would! There would be nothing to say because I would know everything already. I wouldn't have anything to learn because they wouldn't bring anything new to the table. Nothing would be exciting; nothing would be fresh. We would all be the same.

Differences are good. Without them, life would be one-dimensional. We need to start looking at one another's unique interests and characteristics as *cool* because really, what makes us all different from one another are often our most charming qualities. We must embrace and respect these differences instead of labeling or judging them. It's cool to be different; it's not cool to be like everyone else. We have to allow people to shine and be themselves, because isn't that what we all really want? The freedom to be ourselves and have people support and accept us in the process.

BE TRUE TO YOU

At the end of the day, you and me and your best friend and your arch nemesis all have the same goal: to be happy. In order to be happy, we have to be ourselves. We can make that a whole lot easier by not making fun of things that bring other people happiness, just as we wouldn't want them to do to us. Whether you like to collect certain items, make YouTube videos, create do-it-yourself projects, or play a certain instrument or sport, if it brings you happiness—keep doing it! That's awesome. It doesn't matter what anyone else says. *They* are not *you*. They have their interests and you have yours. Neither of them is better or cooler than the other.

Do what you love and don't ever change. Because those things about you that bring so much happiness are all a part of the person you are. You are not your clothes or your group of friends or your social status. Those have nothing to do with the real you. You are so much more than that stuff because that's just what it is—*stuff*. Although we are tempted to look for things outside ourselves to increase our happiness, they only ever give us a temporary boost and then we're searching for the next thing. That's when we start comparing ourselves to others… *She looks happy. Maybe if I looked like her, or maybe if I had that outfit, I would be happier.* No, no, and NO. Everything you need in order to be happy is right inside you, but you've been looking in the wrong place. Don't try and be anyone other than you. Be *more* of you, every second of every day. Do what feels right and do what you love. That's the key to happiness. Nothing on the outside is.

I know that during school, it may seem like those who are different are targets, but out in the world, those who are different are embraced. When you graduate from school, you will find that people want to be around dynamic individuals they can learn from. Belonging to a certain group of friends is no longer your safety blanket. Your differences are what make you stand out from the crowd. They will be what get people's attention. People want to know what sets you apart from everyone else. Why should they accept you into that college? Why should they hire you for that position? Why should they choose you for that program? That special thing about you that makes you unique is now your greatest gift.

So have the courage to stand out, even when it gets hard, because once you're out of school, people will absolutely welcome that part of you that you've been hesitant to share. And you never know what possibilities can come from being your authentic self.

SURROUND YOURSELF WITH SUPPORTIVE PEOPLE

While we have all different types of friends and friendships, it's important that we make good decisions about how we share our time and energy. Really good friends, the kind who have unconditional love and acceptance for us, can be extremely hard to find. Whether you're the girl of the hour or the girl in the hot seat, these friends have your back no matter what.

Then there are those friends whose feelings are a little unclear and inconsistent. They seem to like us more when we act a certain way or when things are going well for us. Maybe they are extra friendly when they need something. It feels as if they don't always like us, yet we itch for their approval. We want them to like us *so* badly. Meanwhile, they are the first to turn away when we hit a rough patch.

These girls don't seem as invested in the friendship as we are. And that's not good because one person is made to feel inferior by the other person. They may make us feel uncomfortable about certain parts of our personality or interests. Maybe it's a hobby we have, or a club we are in, or a sport that we play that they don't seem too fond of. Whatever it may be, when they comment on it sarcastically or negatively it makes us feel insecure. Now that *thing* that we love to do that sets us apart and makes us different is suddenly under our scrutiny. How much do we *really* love it? Is it worth still doing it if it's going to push others away?

In that moment, when we start to have those thoughts, we have to STOP them in their tracks before we turn our back on ourselves and do something that we will later regret. And that's giving up something that you love because of what others say. At some point or another, these types of friendships *will* fade out, because they are not based on strong, loyal bonds. We will learn, even if it's a few years later, that we were never really friends with them in the first place.

While we may not always love every single personality quirk about our friends, we cannot only accept this part of them and not accept that part. We cannot only hang with them when things are all good, and then desert them when they hit a bump in the road. We can't only have their backs when everyone loves them, and then stray away when they're the center of a nasty rumor. And we *certainly* cannot put down things that bring them happiness, that is for sure. That's not being a friend. So if any of your "friends" make you feel insecure or uncool over something that lights you up… that is a huge red flag.

I hope you know that this is nothing to be bummed out about, because there are people who love *all* the parts of you.

They are not conditional friends who come and go as they please. These are people you can be 100 percent yourself with and know that they will accept you and support you. These are the people you should be spending your time with. These are the relationships that you should make a priority. Because when the going gets rough, they will be standing right next to you. You need to surround yourself with those people as much as you can.

My next-door neighbor just so happens to be one of those people. Growing up, I lived on a street where there were very few kids. So when Heather moved next door and I found out that she was my age, I was so excited. *Finally, I'm not surrounded by old people,* I thought, in my ten-year-old mind. Heather and I soon became really close and although she wasn't in my immediate group of friends at school, we hung out a lot outside of school. If I had felt let down by a friend, or if I was preoccupied by something going on in school, I could always rely on Heather to be there for me. She was a consistent friend and never judged me or made me feel insecure or inferior. She was someone I could be my complete self with and not have to worry.

Although I knew that at the time, I don't think I realized that she was a *way* better friend to me than most of the girls I was calling my "best friends." It is people and friendships like Heather that you remember for a lifetime. It is those people who, years down the line, you can call them and pick up right where you left off. I only wish that I realized *just* how special of a friend Heather was when I was younger, so we could have been as close in school as we were outside it. And I wish that instead of giving more attention to friendships that weren't always so positive, I could have given it to one that really was.

Sometimes when we know that someone will always be there, we take that relationship for granted. We may take advantage of their kindness or expect them to just always be around. We don't work on our friendship as much because we know that, no matter what, that person loves us, accepts us, and wants to spend time with us. We don't have to try to get them to like us, because they already do.

If you are fortunate enough to have friends like that, it's important to let them know how much you appreciate them. Thank them for being an amazing friend, for being a positive, loving presence in your life. And hang on to them! Hold them close to your heart, and spend as much time with them as you can because that kind of person is rare and special. Those types of friends don't come along every day.

Focus on the good, supportive people in your life. Be a great friend to them and they will continue being that great friend to you, especially when they know how much you notice and appreciate it.

I hope by now you realize just how special you are. I hope you see that your interests, talents, and skills make you vibrant. Embrace them. Share them with others. Love the heck out of them. Have the courage to stand out and not conform. Find the special qualities that set you apart and don't ever be afraid to let them shine. They are your gifts.

Remember, it's cool to be different. It's cool to be *you*. Love and accept the differences in you and love and accept the differences in others so you can all find your own version of happy. And always, always stay true to yourself.

MAKE YOUR MOVE

1. I LOVE MY…

Write down five things that you love about *you*. Forget about other people's opinions or thoughts. Leave behind your insecurities or flaws. What do you love about yourself? It could be a personality trait or a hobby. Maybe you love how kind you are to others and how you're always including your whole group of friends in activities. Or perhaps you love your fashion sense or your dancing skills or your artistic abilities.

It's important that we show ourselves some love because, all too often, we focus on what we don't like about ourselves. We're drinking way too much hater-ade these days and it's time to shift our focus to the positive.

So make your list and post it in a place where you will see it throughout the day. It could be on a bathroom mirror, a closet door, in your locker. Make sure you stop and read it every time you pass by and give yourself a hug while you're at it!

1. OPPOSITES ATTRACT

Choose someone in your grade with whom you think you have absolutely nothing in common. Perhaps it's that girl you've labeled (and now realize why it's best not to do that!) or maybe it's the girl you think is too cool to be your friend. I want you to make a conscious effort to talk with this person a few times this week. Find out her interests and what she likes to do. Learn something about her that you never knew before.

We think we know someone from our external impressions of them, but it's amazing what we discover when we leave behind these judgments and stereotypes and genuinely take the time to get to know someone. Our perceptions change. You may be more similar than you think. And that person could have a really inspiring story and be a phenomenal friend—if we only reach out.

It's important that we don't dismiss people based on what we *think* we know about them. I challenge you to step out of your comfort zone. I guarantee you will be pleasantly surprised!

9 BE YOUR OWN BEST FRIEND

The most important relationship you have in your life is the relationship you have with yourself. Really let that message sink in. While this is not something that we are all taught at a young age or even hear often, the power behind it is truly immeasurable. You are YOU every single second of every day. You spend a lot of time with yourself. How do you treat that person? How do you talk to her? Do you even like her? Some of us might like ourselves and some of us might not. But that is okay because we're going to change that.

While you're entitled to your feelings and opinions, you're also entitled to happiness and you're entitled to love yourself unconditionally. You should be as kind and loving to yourself as you are to your friends and family. For this final chapter, we are going to break down why it's so important to love yourself, and you'll be given all the steps needed to get there. Get ready to send some serious appreciation your way because you're the star of the show…

YOU COME FIRST

Putting yourself first, loving yourself, is the secret ingredient that can take your good life and turn it into a great one. Putting yourself first doesn't mean that you love anyone else less. In fact, loving yourself enables you to love others a whole lot more. Putting yourself first means being KIND to yourself, talking NICELY to yourself, and LOVING yourself. Yes, your first loyalty must be to YOU because if you don't take care of yourself, if you can't love yourself and make yourself happy, how can someone else?

Now, if you're like me, your initial reaction might have included a voice in your head picketing against self-love and telling you the idea is all sorts of crazy. But let's clear the air. Self-love doesn't mean being conceited or self-absorbed. Although on the surface it might seem like people with a lot of self-love are obsessed with themselves, it couldn't be further from the truth. People who appear overly in love with themselves frequently have low confidence or self-esteem that is wayyyy too fragile. They inflate whatever part of themselves they believe is lacking—be it their appearance or their achievements—to disguise their internal discomfort. This can make them seem cocky, often by bragging or being flashy or the like.

On the other hand, people who are genuinely soaking up

the self-love are content and happy with themselves. They are secure in who they are and don't need outside validation to make them feel good. Doesn't that sound appealing?

Are you still hesitating? Are you concerned that the more you love yourself, the less room there is to love others? Don't worry! We are not on a love budget. Love is unlimited. Love cannot be measured. Having more love for ourselves doesn't mean we have less love to give to others. In fact, the more you love yourself, the more you are open to loving others because you are whole, you are happy, you are confident in yourself. Feeling full with love for ourselves allows us to love others more fully.

HEAD OVER HEELS FOR YOU

You have the opportunity to love yourself, your life. Take it! We can't expect to turn into self-loving masters overnight, but this is all about baby steps. Any progress is good progress. Being kind to yourself today is a victory over being critical. Self-love is no walk in the park; it's HARD. Especially in a world that constantly tells us to look a certain way, be a certain type of person, accomplish a certain level of success. You are going to have moments of self-doubt, but that's when you have to remind yourself that self-love isn't about being perfect; it's about accepting and embracing your imperfections. Love grows over time, and you'll get better at it the more you practice.

Hopefully by now you are all warmed up to putting

yourself first and are willing to give self-love a shot. So let's get the ball rolling!

YOUR LOVE LIST

The first thing I want you to do is to grab a paper and pen, and take a few minutes to think about the characteristics that make up a great friend. What are the most important qualities? Think about your own bestie. Is she always there for you? Does she encourage you, support you, and accept you? What happens when you make a negative comment about your appearance or are really down about something? What does she say? I bet she lifts you up and makes you feel better. Take your time making this list because it's going to provide the framework for your new friendship with YOU! Because again, the most important relationship in your life is the relationship you have with yourself!

Next, look at your list and commit to incorporating these traits into your day-to-day interactions with YOU. Do this however works best for you. You can pick one trait a week and make that your mini-goal, layering them on one at a time. Or you can dive in full force and start working on all of them.

For example, if one of the items on your list is being a good listener, take time to check in with yourself. Is something weighing heavily on your mind? If so, literally talk through the problem like you would with a friend who calls you when she is upset.

From this day on, strive to treat yourself like the

awesome person who you are. Because if you're being unkind and hating on yourself, that's how others will treat you too. But if you love yourself and treat yourself nicely, you'll welcome people into your life who treat you with that same loving kindness.

MAKE A DATE WITH YOU

The next order of business is to pencil some you time onto your calendar. School, homework, extracurricular activities, and friends are all priorities in your life, and self-love should be too! But far too often it is the first thing that gets skipped, especially on a busy day. I would argue, however, that it's actually the most important because it truly changes the kind of day you have.

Setting a daily routine is golden. Keep it consistent if you can. For example, pick a time every day and schedule a date with yourself! You may be wondering what to do. Well, there are no rules! Get creative.

Personally, mornings really set the tone for my day. If I am woken up early by the oh-so-annoying sound of my alarm, only to rush around at lightning speed to get ready for a FULL day ahead of me, I'll feel completely chaotic. On the other hand, if I give myself an extra ten minutes to read something positive and uplifting while I eat breakfast, I feel like I'm starting my day off on the right foot. That way I get to set the tone for my day, rather than feeling like the day is controlling me. That's why I make sure to take my self-love time in the morning. It really makes a difference!

However you decide to fill your time is up to you, but it shouldn't feel like a burden. In fact, your self-love appointment should boost you and make you feel connected to YOU. Perhaps you keep a gratitude journal where you write things you are thankful for. This is an awesome way to keep focused on the positive. Or maybe you start your day by saying: "I love you, (insert your name here)!" It might be a little uncomfortable at first, but that just goes to show how you might have been slacking in the be-kind-to-yourself department. (Believe me, you're not the only one!) Another suggestion is revisiting activities from previous chapters. Maybe do something on your mood-booster list or leave positive quotes around your room, as mentioned in chapter two. Focus on what makes you happy and make time for that. And don't forget to shoot yourself some compliments!

Lastly, it's important to remember that your "me date" can fit your mood. If you're having a bad day, your self-love time could involve collecting your thoughts and simply feeling whatever it is you feel. Just make sure to give yourself a hug afterward.

From this day forward, make a promise that the relationship you have with YOU will be important. Just as you give attention and love to the special people in your life, you have to give yourself the love and attention you deserve. You can do it. I believe in you.

So let me ask you one more question: Who is your best friend? (This is where you scream loudly, I AM!!!!)

THE FEAR VOICE

While being our own BFF may sound great in theory, some of us might find it really difficult to get there. And that's because each of us has what I call a fear voice. This is not the voice of reason. In fact, it is quite the opposite. This fear voice will try to convince you to play small. It likes to hold you back and make you think you're not good enough. It tells you that you can't succeed and shouldn't dream. The fear voice is like the world's biggest party pooper. You could be feeling inspired and hopeful, then that voice sweeps in and tells you that you're wrong, that you won't be able to achieve that goal. Way to be a buzzkill, fear voice.

For some of us this voice is a whisper, and for others it's projected through surround-sound speakers. At some point or another, we all have to take responsibility for that voice and the damage that it's creating in our minds, our hearts, and ultimately, our lives. What we do when this voice speaks up is hugely important. Are you going to listen or are you going to tune it out?

Now, it's almost impossible to remove all fear-based thoughts from our minds—but there are things we can do so the fear voice doesn't paralyze us. We can learn to turn down the volume of the fear voice and turn up the volume of our love voice. Because it is that loving voice that will make us happy and encourage us to do great things.

So anytime you hear that fear and negative self-talk are creeping into your thoughts, call them out and shut it down.

Combat that fear-based thought with a loving one. If your fear voice is making you think that you won't fit in, choose not to believe it. Instead, change that thought the moment in enters your mind. Tell yourself that people will love and accept you because you are an absolutely incredible person. Notice your most common fear-voice statements and literally replace them with their loving opposite. If fear tells you that you can't do something, remind yourself that you are so talented and say, "Actually, I can."

While we're on the topic of "I cant's," allow me to suggest ditching that phrase all together. "I can't" is one of the most debilitating statements a person can make because it literally blocks you. We say it so frequently that it almost becomes an automatic response. We make up our minds that we can't do something before we even give it a try.

But remember what we said about setting limits? What would happen, worst-case scenario, if you aren't as successful as you'd like? Yes, you may feel embarrassed or make a silly mistake, but so much of that is in our own head. Other people don't really care whether we are experts at something or not.

For the next few days, observe how often you're saying, "I can't." Whenever you catch yourself, try and pinpoint why exactly you think you can't. I bet, when it comes down to it, there is a part of you that is scared to fail. It's that fear voice talking.

But you know what? You are not alone. Failure is scary for everyone. There is NOTHING wrong with failure.

Failure will always teach us something. You learn, through failure, how you can do things differently, do things better. FEAR of failure holds you back from taking risks, taking a leap of faith, following your heart. Do not let the fear of failure keep you from achieving your dreams. You have to believe that you are enough, that you are worthy of happiness, success, and love because you truly are. You were born to shine. That's not just true for some of us. It's true for ALL of us. This is your life—be what you want, be who you want, go after the things that bring you the greatest joy. Take risks. You have it in you to be, do, and have everything you desire. And if you stay true to yourself and go after those goals with all of your heart, you will live a life beyond your wildest dreams.

LOVE YOURSELF NOW

Too often we focus on what we want to change about ourselves, calling out our flaws and wishing we were a little different than the person we actually are. Some of us may paint a picture in our minds of our "perfect self"…the ideal image of who we want to be, of how we want to look and act. Instead of loving ourselves for who we are right this very instant, we take a rain check, saving that love for when we become the idealized person we imagine.

But no one is perfect! And that's totally okay. The person you are now deserves all the love you have to give. Don't hold out on yourself. You, my friend, are far more wonderful than you realize… sweatpants, messy hair, and all.

We've all compared our appearance, intelligence, personality, wardrobe, and countless other things to how the people around us look and what they have, zeroing in on the areas where we are "lacking." We've pinpointed, dissected, and obsessed over what we think is wrong with ourselves. We've been our own worst critics. But we owe it to ourselves to GET OFF OUR OWN BACKS!

Don't get me wrong, I'm all for hopping on the self-improvement train when there are areas we need to work on. Yet when we critique ourselves more than we love ourselves, we become our own bullies. And it's time to change that.

Imagine how it would feel to eliminate all of this judgmental behavior. How much happier would we be if we focused on all we like about ourselves? We may never be the most popular, the most gorgeous, the most success-ful, or the most athletic. But those things don't guarantee happiness anyway. What we can be, however, is the most kind, the most loving, and the most accepting to ourselves.

As you continue down this self-love journey, there are going to be times when you make mistakes or you're not so proud of something that you said or did. You're human. You're allowed to mess up. But how you treat yourself, and others, when that happens is just as important as how you treat yourself, and others, when all is good. It's important to cut yourself some slack now and again. Just because you are having a bad day, a bad week, doesn't mean you are any less amazing or deserving of love. It just means you hit a bump in the road. Forgive yourself and get back on track.

Your job—and the greatest gift you can give to yourself—is to love and accept yourself. Embrace your appearance. You are beautiful. Embrace your personality. You are unique. Embrace your talents and strengths. Own them! You are, by every definition, amazing and cool. Even on an ordinary day, extraordinary things can happen. Don't rely on others for those magical moments. Create that magic for yourself!

MAKE YOUR MOVE

Instead of focusing on what we don't like about ourselves and being our own worst critics, we should love ourselves, compliment ourselves, and encourage ourselves. Sure, you will make mistakes. Everyone does. But treat yourself like you would like to be treated. Be kind; be gentle; be supportive. You are pretty incredible, so love who you are. You are truly dazzling.

1. DEAR ME

Write a letter to yourself, reflecting on the insights you have gained while reading this book. This is your chance for a fresh start. What positive changes do you want to make?

Perhaps you want to be more self-loving and accepting or maybe you are inspired to reach out to make new friends or stop gossiping. Whatever you feel you could improve on, write it down. When we make a promise to our self and write it down, it becomes more official—and it makes it easier to hold ourselves accountable.

Be sure to sign your letter, then fold it up and put it somewhere safe. Revisit your letter from time to time. Applaud yourself for the efforts you are taking to be kind to yourself and to others. And when you feel like you are deviating from your promise, reopen the letter to remind yourself of what you wrote. It will help you refocus.

Remember: be gentle with yourself. Every day is a chance to try again. You are a work in progress. It takes immense courage and strength to own our mistakes and take positive action. There is nothing cooler than a girl who is honestly herself, flaws and all. And you, my friend, are very, very cool.

1. LOVE YOU, NO MATTER WHAT.

Promise to love yourself, always, no matter what. Some days may be more challenging than others, but you can overcome any obstacle, so create a list to remind yourself. Put a header on the top of the page that says, "I will love myself…" and below it, include examples, starting each line with "regardless of."

I will love myself…

regardless of how other people treat me.

regardless of my accomplishments.

regardless of my body shape and appearance.

regardless of my love life's status.

regardless of my popularity.

regardless of my material possessions.

Keep the list flowing. Because from here on out, loving yourself is nonnegotiable. You should wake up every morning and love yourself simply because you are YOU and that person is pretty unbelievable. (Look back at your "I Love My…" list from the previous chapter when you need a reminder!) Don't let another day go by when you're not appreciating yourself or being kind to yourself. Don't wait to show yourself some love; love yourself NOW.

Thank you so much for joining me on this journey! I've enjoyed leading you through the ins and outs of Girl World. I hope this book will help you get through challenging moments, that it will guide you and give you the advice you need. School can be a really fun place, but it can also be difficult. Let this book be a source of comfort for you. Revisit it whenever you need a little soul boost. You are not alone in your feelings. So many of us girls understand exactly what you're going through, and we have your back.

But most of all, I hope this book inspires you to make positive choices—and reminds you that you are nothing short of incredible. You have everything you already need to lead a life beyond your wildest dreams. Stay true to yourself and dream big.

We may have reached the end of the book, but don't

go radio silent on me! Come say hello and stay in touch. I'd love to hear from you! Visit me at sistersoldier.org or connect with me on Instagram (@sister_soldier) and Facebook (Facebook.com/SisterSoldierStandUp).

It's time to say good-bye to the drama and let your inner amazing shine through. That will ALWAYS, always lead you to happiness.

With love,

Trish

ACKNOWLEDGMENTS

First and foremost, I would like to thank my family. Mom, you are my soul mate. I would never be the person I am today without having you as my mother. Thank you for your kind, beautiful heart and for teaching me the true meaning of love. Dad, you have always believed in me and have supported me in every decision I have made. I cherish our bond and love you dearly. To my brother, Lorenzo, thank you for being someone that I look up to and someone I can always rely on. I love you so much and I am so proud of you. Cristina—there are no words to describe how I feel about you. You are not only my sister but also my closest friend. Thank you for your unconditional love, support, and encouragement. You are an amazing person and one of the biggest blessings in my life.

To my angels: Grandma Menendez, Grandpa Ottaviano, Abuela, and Uncle Ralph, I love you and miss you every day. And to Ben Breedlove, I hold your story close to my heart. Thank you for inspiring me and making my life better.

To my mentor, Gabrielle Bernstein—I am forever changed because of you. Thank you for transforming my life and for helping me manifest my dreams. I love you and am so grateful for you!

To Macha Einbender—one phone conversation with you changed my life. Starting Sister Soldier and every miracle that has stemmed from it is a direct result of your belief in me. I am so thankful to have met you.

To the friends that I have had along the way…thank you for being a part of my journey and for the lessons that you have taught me. To the friends that I have today, thank you for your love and support. You inspire me every day!

Ari Pappas—you are a ray of sunshine. Thank you for your constant encouragement and the joy, love, and laughter you bring into my life.

To those who have helped create this book, thank you for believing in this message! To my literary agent, Steve Harris, thank you for the countless phone conversations that we have had and for patiently answering *all* of my questions! To my editor, Annette Pollert-Morgan, and the entire Sourcebooks Fire family, I am blessed and grateful to have worked with you on this project!

To every girl I have met through Sister Soldier—you are my inspiration behind this book. Thank you for your courage and honesty and thank you for sharing your stories with me!

Lastly, thank you to all those involved in antibullying efforts and in raising awareness about this cause. I admire your work and I thank you for making the world a better and kinder place.

ABOUT THE AUTHOR

Photo by Chia Messina

Patricia is the founder of the national nonprofit organization Sister Soldier—Stand Up For Each Other, a school assembly and empowerment program geared directly toward middle and high school girls who are negatively affected by female aggression and bullying. Inspired by her own middle school experience, this young author and speaker sets out to empower teen girls, all across the country, with kindness, acceptance, and self-confidence, ultimately changing the way they view themselves and view each other. Patricia graduated from the University of Michigan with bachelors degrees in psychology and communications and holds a master's degree in school psychology. She lives in New York City.

Sister
SOLDIER

STAND UP FOR EACH OTHER

Be different. Be *YOU.*

Stand UP for yourself. Stand UP for each other.

Change your life. Love your life.

LIVE YOUR LIFE.

To learn more or invite Trish to visit your school,
visit Sistersoldier.org.

PEACE
RESPECT
TRUST
LOVE
LAUGH
FORGIVE
BELIEVE
INSPIRE
HOPE
FRIENDSHIP
CHANGE

Be inspired
by Patricia Ottaviano's

Girl World

From Sourcebooks Fire